# NATURAL LAW
## or
# Don't Put A Rubber On Your Willy

*by Robert Anton Wilson*

**LOOMPANICS UNLIMITED**
Port Townsend, Washington

*WARNING:*
*THE ATTORNEY GENERAL HAS DETERMINED*
*THAT THIS BOOK MAY BE HAZARDOUS TO*
*YOUR DOGMA*

*This book is sold for information purposes only. Neither the author nor the publisher will be held accountable for the use or misuse of the information contained in this book.*

## NATURAL LAW
## OR DON'T PUT A RUBBER ON YOUR WILLY
© 1987 by Loompanics Unlimited

**Published by:**
Loompanics Unlimited
P.O. Box 1197
Port Townsend, WA 98368
Loompanics Unlimited is a division of Loompanics Enterprises, Inc.

ISBN 0-915179-61-X
Library of Congress Catalog Card Number 86-82892

*The laws of God, the laws of Man*
*He may keep who will, and can;*
*Not I: let God and Man decree*
*Laws for themselves and not for me.*

—A.E. Housman

**Robert Anton Wilson** is a novelist, poet, playwright, lecturer, stand-up comic, Futurist and psychologist. In science-fiction, he is the co-author (with Robert Shea) of the *Illuminatus* trilogy, which won the 1986 Prometheus Hall of Fame Award, and author of the *Schroedinger's Cat* trilogy (called "the most scientific of all science-fiction novels" by *New Scientist.)* Among his historical novels are *The Earth Will Shake, The Widow's Son* and *Masks of the Illuminati.* Wilson holds a Ph.D. in psychology from Hawthorn University, edited the "Playboy Forum" department of *Playboy* for six years, and regularly gives seminars at Esalen and other New Age centers. His nonfiction works of Futurist psychology and guerrilla ontology include *Prometheus Rising* and *Right Where You Are Sitting Now.* His latest books are a novel, *Nature and Nature's God,* and a polemic against Fundamentalist Materialism, *The New Inquisition.* Wilson has made a comedy record (*Secrets of Power*), a Punk Rock record (*The Chocolate Biscuit Conspiracy*) and was recently a guest of the Norwegian government at the Oslo International Poetry Festival. He resides in Ireland, and his play, *Wilhelm Reich in Hell,* was recently performed at the Edmund Burke Theatre in Dublin.

# TABLE OF CONTENTS

Political Myth and Self-Hypnosis .................... 1

The Wrath of Rothbard ........................... 4

Smith *Ex Cathedra* ................................ 9

"Law" in Science and Theology .................... 10

Faith and Deep Belief ............................ 17

Metaphysics Without "God" ....................... 22

Natural Law as Ventriloquism ..................... 28

On Sodomizing Camels ........................... 33

What Is "Against Nature?" ........................ 39

Why Not "Violate" Nature? ....................... 45

The Individual vs. the Abstract ................... 54

Toward a Conclusion Almost ..................... 58

Sleep-Walking and Hypnotism ..................... 62

# POLITICAL MYTH
# AND SELF-HYPNOSIS

*A rose by any other name*
*Would never, never smell the same*
*And cunning is the nose that knows*
*An onion that's been called a rose.*

— Wendell Johnson, *Your Most Enchanted Listener*

Nobody ever wins a debate with an editor in his own magazine, for the same reason that nobody has ever persuaded the Pope of his own fallibility.

Three years ago, Loompanics published *The Myth of Natural Rights* by L.A. Rollins. In 1985, the *New Libertarian* magazine (1515 W. MacArthur Blvd, #19, Costa Mesa, CA 92626) published extensive debate on the very interesting issues Rollins raised. I participated in that debate, and the experience was enlightening, although not in the Zen Buddhist sense. Briefly, the editor, Samuel Edward Konkin III, did not print my article as I wrote it; instead he printed the article intercut with a running commentary by himself, in the form of numerous footnotes attempting to rebut all my major points.

In the ordinary civilized decorum of debate, a gentleman is expected to wait until his opponent's time is up before replying. Interrupting your opponent continually is called "heckling" and is regarded as boorish and uncivil. I could not regard Konkin's interpolations in my article as anything else but literary heckling, and I was curious. Ordinarily, Konkin seems a civilized person. I wondered about the psychology of the heckler and why it can afflict even the educated person if his or her prejudices are sufficiently affronted.

Basically, I think, the heckler fears his opponent. He thinks that the opponent's ideas are a "clear and present danger," as it were, and that they must be drowned out before they seduce anyone. You generally know when you have trodden upon somebody's deepest prejudices because their civility deserts them and they begin interrupting excitedly and adopting the "heckler" persona.

In thinking this over, and considering also the emotional and almost hysterical nature of other responses during the debate on Natural Law sparked by Rollins, I have realized that there seem to be deep religious passions involved in this issue, and that my article in *New Libertarian* only scratched the surface of the psychology and neurology of the Natural Law cult. I have therefore decided to rewrite my thoughts in more depth and publish them where the Natural Law cultists can only denounce them *after* they have been read and cannot heckle and distract the reader *while* they are being read.

Curiously, while the Natural Law debate was going forth in the *New Libertarian* in the United States, I was involved in two other debates on Natural Law in Ireland, where I live. Dail hEireann, the Irish parliament, had voted to submit to the people a referendum which would have allowed civil divorce if approved by a majority; you will not be surprised to learn that the proposed legislation was violently opposed by the Roman Catholic hierarchy on the grounds that divorce "is" against "Natural Law." At the same time, a neo-pagan Dublin magazine, *Ancient Ways*, was running two debates on whether machinery "was" or "was not" against Natural Law and on whether anti-aging research "is" or "is not" against Natural Law. I participated in both of these debates also, and it became quite clear to me that the Natural Law mystique, in Catholic, libertarian or neo-pagan forms, remains basically a set of rhetorical strategies to *hypnotize* oneself and try to *hypnotize* others into the state which Bernard Shaw called "barbarism" and defined as "the belief that the laws of one's own tribe are the laws of the universe."

The word "hypnotize" is not used lightly in the above sentence.

I shall endeavor to show, in these pages, that the Natural Law metaphysics can accurately be described as a verbal construct that, like a hypnotist's commands, creates a trance state in which experience is edited out and the verbally-

2

induced hypnotic revery becomes more "real" than sensory-sensual stimuli. In other words, Natural Law appears to be a map that does not correspond to any real territory, but like other Idols it becomes almost "real" when the worshipper stares at it long enough with passionate adoration. Like Catholic statues of Mary, it will even seem to "move" or "come alive."

I shall also attempt to show that this kind of trance should be considered statistically "normal" because most people most of the time are similarly entranced by word-and-symbol hypnosis and self-hypnosis. We appear to be a race, as Max Stirner said, with "spooks in the head."

This claim is not intended as polemic, but as sober diagnosis. I shall demonstrate as we proceed that hypnosis occurs quite ordinarily in human affairs and is easily induced by the repetition of metaphysical chants and other meaningless verbalisms.

A hypnotist tells you that now you are going away from this room, far away, and now you are in a lovely green field, and it is a warm summer day, and the sun is all over your body....you can feel the warm sun all over your body, and it is very relaxing....very relaxing....and now you hear the sound of a very beautiful bird call...

And, of course, if the hypnosis works, you *do* hear the bird call.

Similarly, the Natural Law theorist (or any other metaphysician) tells you about abstractions with capital letters, and he talks about these marvelously transcendental entities, and he talks, and he talks....and if the hypnosis works, the abstractions suddenly seem as "real" as, *or even more "real" than,* a ham sandwich and a cup of coffee. The process of going away from sensory-sensual experience into verbally-induced fantasy works the same way in both forms of hypnosis, as we shall see.

3

# THE WRATH OF ROTHBARD

*Truth! Truth! Truth! crieth the Lord of The Abyss of Hallucinations*

—Aleister Crowley, *The Book of Lies*

In *New Libertarian*, Vol. 4, No. 13, Prof. Murray Rothbard published an article called "On the Duty of Natural Outlaws to Shut Up." In it, Rothbard "replied" to Rollins's *The Myth of Natural Rights*, more or less, although he did not answer any of the very telling criticisms Rollins had leveled against his (Rothbard's) claim that some sort of metaphysical entity called a "right" resides in a human being like a "ghost" residing in a haunted house. Nevertheless, Rothbard's article seemed to me a very forceful polemic and had the same emotional power, and indeed the same logical structure, as a marvelous sentence attributed to Ring Lardner:

*"Shut up," he explained.*

The persuasiveness of such "explanations" can be considerable, especially if they are delivered in a loud voice and accompanied by a threatening gesture with a baseball bat. In Rothbard's article, however, they are accompanied only by the literary equivalent of such noise and threat, i.e., by what semanticists call "snarl words" — words which express mammalian rage but do not contain information.

It seems part of our glorious primate heritage that such noise and threat is often mistaken for argument, even though it should more properly be called quarrel. Politicians, advertisers and, above all, the rev. clergy have been very

4

industrious in spreading the notion that there is no difference between noise and information and that loud noise is itself informative. It is no surprise, in this mammalian context, that Rothbard actually includes in his piece the helpful suggestion that the appropriate response to certain annoying questions is to hit the questioner with a chair.

As I say, I do not deny the vigor of such rhetoric, but I find it lacking in intellectual coherence. I do discern a kind of a trace of an adumbration of a hint of an argument in the midst of Rothbard's territorial howls, but I cannot be perfectly sure I have grasped it, since the noise of Rothbard's rage tends to drown out the content of whatever he is trying to say.

I have given you the date and place of Rothbard's publication of his thesis; you can look it up for yourself to see if there is more content in it than I have found. Meanwhile, it seems to me that his major assertion is that stupidity is the best and quickest way to political success, and that those who are not really stupid should at least pretend to be stupid, since dishonesty is almost as good as stupidity if you practice it long enough and hard enough. Now I do not disagree with this at all; indeed, my own analysis of politics and political Ideologies appears to be exactly the same. The only difference seems to be that I have just stated it as bluntly and cynically as possible, whereas Rothbard states it with a great deal of unction or lubricating oil, to make it go down more smoothly.

What Rothbard actually says (in part) is "What moves men and women and changes history is ideology, moral values, deep beliefs and principles" and "moral passions and ideology *work* and pragmatism doesn't," and that one who is not a moralist in this sense should "pretend to be a moralist" since that is good Public Relations. I do not think my sarcastic paraphrase above was unjustified. Some of us, however, agree with John Adams that Ideology should more properly be called idiocy: we harbour the suspicion that the "deep beliefs" and "moral passions" associated with Ideologies tend to make people behave like lunatics (or like badly-wired robots) and that strong doses of skepticism and down-to-earth pragmatism appear to be the only factors that have ever produced any relative sanity or relative peace anywhere. We

5

agree that passionate ideology and "deep" belief (i.e. deliberate blindness) indeed makes for political success and has created history as we know it; *but that is precisely why we find politics and history so terrible to contemplate.*

John Adams, looking at the effects of Ideology, said he could not consider history without either laughing or weeping. Most of us, these days (except the Ideologists), feel that way; like James Joyce, we regard history as a nightmare from which we are trying to wake. Like Joyce, we have learned to "fear those big words that make us so unhappy." We have looked at the victims of "moral passion" and "deep belief" (which we are more likely to call fanaticism) and we have become agnostic, somewhat cynical and very, very cautious about that kind of passion and that kind of belief.

So, then, if I were interested in entering ordinary politics, in the framework of the rules of ordinary history, I would follow Rothbard's advice, "shut up" (as he urges) about my philosophical doubts, and pretend to the kind of passion and dogmatic belief that historically always leads to political success. In my view, however, such passionate dogmatism usually makes people stupid — Koestler called it "deliberate stupidity" — and it often makes them blindly cruel. It even appears to some of us that *passionate belief* can justly be called the principle reason politics remains such a depressing, paleolithic and murderous spectacle. That is why I am not interested in *entering* politics at all, but only in satirizing and undermining it, so that others may see it as I do, come to their senses, and grow reasonably pragmatic, a bit more skeptical and relatively sane and peaceful; hence, I will *not* shut up. Sorry, Professor Rothbard.

Of course, Prof. Rothbard has written elsewhere, e.g. in his *For a New Liberty*, a detailed argument for Natural Law in the moral sense. Rollins pointed out severe flaws in that argument — and it is odd that Rothbard does not offer a rebuttal of any kind, except to urge Rollins and people like him to shut up — but I think something of Rothbard's case is worth mentioning here. Basically, Rothbard argues that each "entity" in the world has a "distinct nature" and that the "nature" of each "entity" can be "investigated by reason." He then "investigates" the nature of "man" by reasoning from

6

abstract definitions and determines what "man's nature" "is" — nothing is specifically said about "woman" — and this, of course, is the basis for "Natural Law" in the moral sense.

While Rollins has made hash of the logical connections in Rothbard's argument, I wish to point out merely that Rothbard bases himself entirely on the categories of medieval (pre-scientific) philosophy. Aristotle originated and Thomas Aquinas developed the idea of the world made up of "entities" each possessing an indwelling "nature," which can be known by abstract reasoning from abstract definitions. This survives in the Cartesian philosophy of "the ghost in the machine," because Descartes assumed block-like mechanisms, instead of block-like entities, but left them still haunted by spiritual essences. We shall return to this point in detail, but for now it is enough to mention that science has not employed this Aristotelian-Thomist-Cartesian model for over 300 years. Science does not assume "natures" spookily indwelling "within" things, at all, at all. Science posits functional relations between "things" or events. These functional relations can also be called patterned coherencies or, in Bucky Fuller's terminology, "knots" — energy patterns and interferences between energies. All scientific models describe such energy "knots" *between* "things" and not spookily indwelling "within" "things." Science also increasingly doubts the existence of "things" in the Thomist sense and speaks more of relations between *space-time events.* I am not asserting that science has "refuted" the Aristotelian-Thomist model, but just that science has found that model useless in discussing the sensory-sensual world of space-time. In other words, even if the Aristotelian-Thomist model refers to something, it does not refer usefully to our existential experience and experiments in space-time. The Aristotelian-Thomist model, as we shall see, refers to some ghostly realm "above" or outside of space-time.

Science, incidentally, not only ignores the question of indwelling "essences" by looking instead at measurable relationships, but science also does not agree that knowledge is obtained through Rothbard's medieval "investigation by reason," i.e., by *inventing* definitions and then deducing what your definitions implicitly assumed. Science investigates by *experiment.* We shall shortly see what a major difference that

7

makes. For now it is sufficient to note that the multiplicity of geometrical and logical systems produced by mathematicians in the last 100 years indicates that you can arrive at any conclusion imaginable by *inventing* definitions that tacitly imply that conclusion: but only experiment gives any indication whether such systems connect at any point with our experiences in space-time. We shall return to this point frequently. Meanwhile, I want to emphasize that, just as the terminology of "Natural Law" derives from medieval Catholicism, Rothbard's defense of this metaphysical doctrine derives also from the medieval Catholic philosophy of indwelling essences. His entire system seems curiously innocent of any taint of the scientific revolution that has occurred since Galileo.

Of course, if you want to engage in abstract metaphysical reasoning about Platonic or Aristotelian realms, where spooks like "Natural Law" may dwell, then you probably have to employ some form of medieval model containing ghostly realms beyond space-time *created by definition and/or axiom.* I am arguing only that if we want to consider our actual situation within space-time, it seems wiser to investigate by experiment those concrete events that can be observed and studied within space-time.

# SMITH *EX CATHEDRA*

*Convictions cause convicts.*

—Malaclypse the Younger, *Principia Discordia*


George H. Smith, in "Roughing Up Rights" (also in *New Libertarian*, Vol. 4, No. 13) has another go at demolishing relativism and skeptical heresy. He presents a set of assertions, uttered *ex cathedra* as it were, and cites Aristotle and Aquinas as if he were addressing an audience of 13th Century monks and those Mighty Names would settle the issue once and for all. Nowhere does he offer us an argument — although he assures us that he will present arguments later, if anybody wants to debate with him.

I will return to Smith's sketch of a possible argument as we proceed: here I will comment only that Rothbard and Smith in tandem make an egregious combination. Rothbard says we doubters should shut up and Smith warns that he is getting his intellectual ammunition in readiness to blast us utterly if we *don't* shut up, and to anybody impressed by resonant rhetoric it probably looks as if they have driven the unbelievers from the field by uttering fierce war-whoops and waving wooden swords. Sure, such nefarious noises would scare the lice off a Viking, as the Irish say.

However, as those archetypal experts on "moral passion" and "deep belief," the rev. gentlemen of the Holy Inquisition, learned eventually, we heretics can be stubborn bastards. I refuse to retire from the field. I will now offer some war-whoops of my own; I hope the judicious will find them to contain more common sense and less noise than the fulminations of Rothbard and Smith.

9

# "LAW" IN SCIENCE & THEOLOGY

*Insofar as the laws of mathematics are certain, they do not refer to reality, and insofar as they refer to reality, they are not certain.*

—Albert Einstein, quoted by Korzybski in *Science and Sanity*

To begin with, since I am not as clever as Rothbard and Smith, I am not as certain as they are.

I offer my opinions *as opinions*, not as dogmas, and I do not claim to refute absolutely the particular deity (or idol) called Natural Law that Rothbard, Smith and kindred intellects are offering for our worship. I am agnostic about that god, as about all gods, but I am not smart enough to be an atheist, as Smith is, or thinks he is. (I suspect, and will argue here, that Smith has merely replaced one Idol with another.) I remain open to the possibility that the divinity called Natural Law exists somewhere, in some sense, as the other idols offered by other theologians may exist somewhere, in some sense. Since I lack precognition, I cannot know what might be discovered tomorrow, or in a hundred years, or in a millenium. All I can say is that, for a slow learner like me, the question of gods and other metaphysical entities including "Natural Law" remains still open at present even if some devoutly insist that it is closed; and that arguments like "Shut up" and "I'll prove it later" only add to my doubts and suspicions.

"Natural Law" in the sense of ideologists or idolators seems quite distinct from "Natural Law" in the sense of the physical sciences. A so-called natural law in the physical sciences is not a law in the legal sense at all, but a statistical or mathematical generalization from which predictions are deduced that can be, in principle, *refuted* by experiment. No experiments can ever *prove* the generalizations of science, *because we do not know and cannot know what surprises future experiments may hold;* but a generalization of science gets to be called a "law" — carelessly and inaccurately, many scientists now feel — when it has survived a great deal of experimental testing over a long period of time. In common sense, such generalizations certainly appear relatively safe and relatively probable; but because we do not know the results of future experiments, generalizations from the past are never *certain.* On the other hand, experiments may *refute* a scientific generalization, which is why the *possibility of refutation* is considered part of the criteria of "meaning" in science. This point is discussed further in the works of Wittgenstein, P.W. Bridgman and Karl Popper, among others, and those seeking further detail are there referred; for now, it is enough to emphasize that the propositions of theology are not considered scientifically "meaningful" because they are so defined as to negate the possibility of refutation — to evade experimental testing entirely.

For instance, the Roman Catholic dogma of trans-substantiation holds that, once blessed by an "ordained priest," a piece of bread becomes *in essence* the body and blood of a Jew who died 2000 years ago. While Rationalists laugh and Catholics grow defensive, the modern scientist pronounces the case "meaningless" because it never can be tested or refuted. The expression "in essence" indeed appears to have been invented to evade experiments. In Thomist theology, the "essence" of a "thing" is by definition not to be known by the senses or by instruments; everything that can be known by the senses or instruments is only "accident," not "essence" in this word-game. From the instrumental or scientific point of view, then, it makes no difference if the "essence" is said to be the body and blood of Christ, or the hide of the Easter Bunny, or the skeleton of The Dong With The Luminous Nose, or all three at once. Since such ghostly or spooky "essences" may theoretically exist or at least may be *asserted* to exist where our instruments only detect *bread*, any number of such theoretical "essences" may be there, even an infinite number, or no "essence" may be there at all. Since there is no scientific way of measuring that which has been

11

defined as immeasurable, there is no scientific meaning in saying either that one "essence" exists in the bread or that a million exist or that none exist at all.

The same criticism applies, of course, to the indwelling "natures" posited by medieval theologians and still posited today by Professor Rothbard. We cannot meaningfully say that they exist or that they do not exist. All that we can say is that they lack meaning in science, since they do not refer to sensory-sensual events observable in space-time.

Thus, one may fill a page with propositions like "All round squares are essentially divine," "All colorless green ideas are essentially diabolical," "All gremlins eat invisible cabbage," etc. and some may find, or think they find, as much comfort and spiritual nourishment in this as Catholics find in the "invisible essence of Christness" in something that looks and tastes like any other piece of bread, or that Prof. Rothbard finds in his indwelling "natures" within "entities." But all such propositions, since they cannot be tested, remain strictly meaningless according to the rules of the science game.

A scientifically meaningful generalization deals with events that can be observed by humans, even if it requires special instruments to observe them. Things that can never be observationally detected even in principle, do not have any scientific meaning.

What of things that can be observed in principle someday, but cannot be observed today? That is, what of statements like "There is a planet with humanoid intelligences in the system of the double star Sirius"? This is not scientifically meaningful today, but it is not meaningless either, since we can in principle visit Sirius in the future and investigate the matter. The modern tendency in science is to class such propositions, not yet meaningful but not forever meaningless, as *indeterminate* statements. Only those statements which even in principle can never be tested are considered totally meaningless — such as our examples of bread that appears to be bread but isn't *essentially* bread, or round squares, or colorless green ideas, or indwelling "natures."

Some claim — indeed Samuel Edward Konkin III claimed in his footnotes to my original article on this subject — that there are scientific propositions that are not instrumental or observational in this sense. Specifically, Konkin cites the propositions of praxeology, such as "Causality exists." This, however, should be considered a proposition in philosophy, not in science; and the main stream of modern science regards praxeology as being as meaningless as theology. Amusingly, the very word "praxeology" comes from *praxis*, which in Latin designated the *customary* way of doing things, i.e., the tribal game-rules. The search for causality once was a rule of the science game, in early times, when it was thought that scientific generalizations must be stated as cause-and-effect mechanisms; but we now know that science can function with or without the causality rule. Some models are stated in causal language, and some are not, and that is all modern science can say about causality. That "causality exists" — in itself and not as a rule of the Classical Physics game — is not a scientific statement, but a game-rule of Aristotelian logic; and, in the most advanced part of modern physics — quantum mechanics — it is generally assumed that causality does *not* exist on the deeper levels of the energy systems that make up an atom. (We will return to this point.) A scientific generalization or *model* may or may not happen to be in causal language, but the model itself is not regarded as absolute or divine: it is regarded as a useful tool *at present*, and it is assumed that it will be replaced by a more useful model in the future.

In summation, scientific models consist of mathematical generalizations that presently appear useful. The habit of calling these models "laws" is increasingly falling into disfavor, and the working philosophy of most scientists is frankly called "model agnosticism." This attitude is that our models can be considered good, relatively, if they have survived many tests, but none are *certain* or *sacred*, and all will be replaced by better models eventually. Models that cannot be tested at all, even in principle, are regarded as meaningless, or as the Logical Positivists used to say, "abuse of language."

"Natural Law" in the scientific sense is, thus, an old-fashioned concept, and one seldom hears working scientists talking about "natural laws" anymore. In fact, what they are inclined to say is more like "This is the model that makes

13

most sense to me right now." Physicists, especially of the Copenhagen philosophy, regard "law" as an unfortunate term in itself, redolent of theology, and consciously banish the word from their vocabulary.

A scientific "law" — when the word is still used — does not imply a law-giver and has nothing in common with "law" in ordinary speech or Statute Law.

"Natural Law" in the moral and theological sense appears shockingly different from this scientific philosophy in every respect.

To take a typical example which has aroused considerable hilarity in this century, the theological "Natural Law" that most astounds us skeptics is that Roman Catholic statute which the Monty Python group has succinctly and colloquially stated as "Don't put a rubber on your willy." In the more resonant and stentorian language the Vatican prefers, this is more usually stated as "Contraception is against Natural Law." One immediately sees that this has nothing in common with those statistical generalizations *metaphorically called "laws"* in science. The Vatican "law" is not subject to experiment; experiment, and refutation by experiment, are simply not relevant to it. The Pope knows, as well as you or I know, that many human males do, in fact, often put rubbers on their willies. That doesn't matter. This kind of "law" does not refer to physical, palpable events.

Ohm's "law" (so-called) holds that E=IR or voltage equals current times resistance. This must be considered a statistical statement, and I came to understand that very keenly while working for five years as a technical laboratory aide in an engineering firm. According to Ohm's law, if current is 2 amperes and resistance is 5 ohms, then voltage will be 2 x 5 or 10 volts. It seldom is, *exactly*. More often it is something like 9.9 volts or 10.1 volts, but I have seen it wander as far as 10.8 volts. The explanations are "instrument error," "human error" and the fact that conditions in a real laboratory are never those of the Ideal (Platonic) Laboratory, just as a real chair is never exactly the Ideal Platonic chair and real horseshit isn't Ideal Platonic Horseshit. (For those who did not have the dubious benefit of education in classical philosophy, it should be explained that, according to Plato, every chair we encounter in sensory-sensual experience "is" an imperfect copy of the Ideal Chair somewhere outside space-time. From this I long ago deduced that every horse encountered and endured in space-time is also an imperfect copy of the Ideal Platonic Horse and all the horseshit I have ever stepped in is just an imperfect copy of Ideal Platonic Horseshit. I'm sure some Platonists have thought of this before me, and not only believe in the Ideal Platonic Horseshit but have religious ecstasies in which they can actually smell it. We will return to this subject when we revert to hypnosis-by-words at the end.)

Nonetheless, although engineers will agree with what I have just written — the only things most engineers believe in are Murphy's Law ("If anything can go wrong with a machine, it will") and Heinlein's Law ("Murphy was an optimist — things go wrong even when they *can't*") — nobody wants to give up Ohm's "law," which remains still a safe statistical generalization, which is all a reasonable person expects in this chaotic universe. If "law" in the scientific sense was like "Natural Law" in the theological sense, one would find the meters reading anything from one volt to a million volts in the above case, and I would be as skeptical about science as I am about theology. But as long as the meters only wobble a little, and Ohm's generalization remains statistically approximately on target, we vulgar pragmatists will accept Ohm's "law," if not as an Eternal Metaphysical Epiphany, then as a useful intellectual tool, or model, and that is good enough for unmetaphysical lowlifes like us.

To turn the comparison around for greater clarity, if theological "Natural Law" was remotely like scientific "law," one would not find millions and millions of men every year successfully yanking condoms over their phalloi; one would find instead a minor wobble only — a few men here and there who *almost but not quite* get the damned rubber over their willies. And if theological "Natural Law" were subject to refutation by experiment, like scientific models mis-called "laws" are, then this Catholic "law" would have been refuted when the first man anywhere succeeded in getting a rubber all the way over his dingus, just as Simon Newcome's proposed "law" that no craft heavier than air can fly was refuted when

Orville Wright got his airplane off the ground for a few seconds at Kill Devils Hill, Kitty Hawk, North Carolina.

Scientific models refer to experience and can be refuted by experience. Theological dogma does not refer to experience, and it is still a mystery to many of us what it *does* refer to, if it refers to anything.

We will see as we continue that Natural Law in the theological-moral sense, not observable or measurable in space-time, exists in or refers to the same ghostly or extramundane plane where some people go in verbal trance or hypnosis and where there is Ideal Platonic Horseshit in abundant supply.

# FAITH AND DEEP BELIEF

*Doubt everything. Find your own light.*
—Last words of Gotama Buddha, in Theravada tradition

All this has been kindergarten stuff really, but the proponents of T.G.G.N.L. (The Great God Natural Law) all attempt to confuse scientific "laws" or models in the statistical and instrumental sense with theological "laws" as the legislations of some Idol or other, and I am trying to deconfuse and differentiate them.

The basic difference between science and theology has not been stated yet. "Don't put a rubber on your willy" should not really be considered an attempt to approximate a scientific "law." It should be called a law in the legal sense. Just as "55 miles per hour speed limit" on a road sign does not mean that it is impossible to go faster than 55 miles per hour, but rather that the highway patrol will arrest you if they catch you exceeding 55 mph, "Contraception is against Natural Law," or "Don't put a rubber on your willy," does not mean *actually* that condoms will not fit over the human penis, but rather that the Roman Catholic "god" will be extremely pissed off at you if he catches you disobeying his rules. In both these cases — speed limits and contraception — *law* means simply the enactment of a law-maker.

In the case of speed limits, it is prudent to obey, since there is no doubt whatever that the highway patrol appears recurrently in sensory-sensual "reality" or ordinary experience, which is the only "reality" most of us know

17

anything about, and observation and experience strongly support the impression that they love to arrest people. In the case of contraception, it would also be prudent to obey if one was first convinced of the existence in sensory-sensual "reality" or normal space-time of the Catholic "god" and second of the notion that this "god," for some divinely inscrutable reason, has a paranoid obsession with the details of the erotic behavior of domesticated primates; but it makes little sense at all if one is not convinced of the existence in spatio-temporal experience of such a bizarre and sex-obsessed divinity.

Thus, from a skeptical and agnostic (not dogmatically atheistic) point of view, the Catholic doctrine of "Natural Law" seems to be an abstraction and reification of Statute Law *based on sheer bluff*. We can see and observe the highway patrol, and we know something about what happens to people hauled into court by them, but nobody has ever seen the Catholic "god" and the claim that he has a kind of super-jail, worse than any human prison and called "Hell," where he tortures those who rouse his ire, has simply not been proven. Of course, one cannot *disprove* the existence of this "god" and his torture chamber — like the "essences" involved in transsubstantiation, they have been defined so as to be incapable of proof or disproof — but whether or not one is going to be frightened by such bogeys depends on one's willingness to buy a pig in a poke. Since theological propositions are scientifically meaningless, those of us of pragmatic disposition simply won't buy such dubious merchandise. We cannot prove with certitude that those who do buy are being swindled, but we also cannot prove with certitude that something that looks and tastes like bread has miraculously become human flesh either. We reserve judgement, and smile cynically at those who rush forward to invest in such notions. Maybe — remotely — there might be something in such promotions, as there might be something in the talking dogs and the stocks in Arabian tapioca mines that W.C. Fields once sold in his comedies, but we suspect that we recognize a con game in operation. At least, we want to hear the dog talk or see the tapioca ore before we buy into such deals.

At this point, of course, the theologian invokes the virtue of "faith" and Prof. Rothbard will again raise his voice in hymns to the value of "deep belief."

In fact, despite my aggravated case of agnosticism, I am willing to grant the value of "faith" in certain specific cases and within specific contexts. For instance, a great deal of human behavior contains what are called *self-fulfilling prophecies*. If you "believe in yourself" as the books on positive thinking recommend, you will often achieve more than those obsessed with a sense of guilt and inadequacy. Those who study for the exams will probably get above-average marks, while those who "know" they can't pass will not bother to cram and will certainly fail. The good job may or may not go to the best candidate, but it never goes to the person who is so sure of failure that he/she doesn't apply for an interview. I even think that I have observed that Christian Scientists (who believe a happy mind makes a healthy body) tend to live longer and look younger than those with gloomy and pessimistic philosophies.

However, as W.C. Fields — that great Authority on faith and gullibility — once said, "If at first you don't succeed, try and try again. Then give up. No sense being a damned fool about it."

Aristotelian either/or logic appears inadequate and misleading today, because the universe apparently can count above two. In the present case, the habit of arguing "for" or "against" faith appears to be simply Aristotelian dualism carried to absurdity. In common sense, if not hypnotized by a Logician, everybody realizes that faith may be a gamble that is worth taking in many cases, but, as Fields says, there is no sense in being a damned fool about it. When psychologists or other counsellors suggest that we might be happier and more successful if we tried, experimentally, to be less pessimistic and have more faith in ourselves and others, that is usually a gamble worth taking. When we are asked to have faith in the Easter Bunny or in a perpetual motion machine sold in a back alley, the rules of ordinary prudence suggest that somebody thinks we are damned fools and is trying to cash in on our folly.

It also needs to be emphasized that all forms of "faith" that remain relatively sane are *limited by time and context.* I will believe for a given time that "the check is in the mail" or that megadoses of a new vitaminic compound are doing me some good; I will believe, in a given context, that optimism works better than pessimism and that if you treat people nicely most of them will be nice in return. In all such acts of faith, one is conscious of taking a gamble. The kind of "faith" demanded by theology and metaphysics is of a different order entirely, because to have "faith" in a system of ideas — any system — demands that one stop thinking entirely, and if the system is especially baroque (e.g. Soviet communism, Roman Catholicism) it also demands that eventually one stop seeing, hearing, smelling or in any way sensing what is actually happening around one.

It cannot be an accident that such "faith," quite properly called "blind faith" in ordinary speech, is only praised as a virtue by those who profit from it.

So, then: for all I know the Catholic "god" may exist somewhere in some form, but the rhetoric of his worshippers arouses dark suspicions. I therefore return the traditional Scots jury verdict: Not Proven. (I believe that verdict was generally employed when the jury had dark suspicions but not total certitude.) I decline Pascal's Wager (a more elegant form of Rothbard's notion that we should pretend a belief if we have it not) because I am not clever enough to understand such abstrusities and when I am uncertain it seems to me the simple, honest thing to *say* frankly that I am uncertain.

And I don't see any need to *seek* certitude or even *pretend* it, when in experience most of what happens to us is uncertain and/or unpredictable, from remembering what we had for dinner last Wednesday to guessing whether or not our flight will leave the airport on schedule or even to intuiting what the hell our best friends are thinking when they put down the whiskey and stare out the window.

The search for certitude — like the pretence of moral righteousness — appears to me as a medieval habit that should have vanished long ago. None of us knows enough to be certain about anything, usually, and none of us are nearly as "moral" as we feel obliged to pretend we are in order to be acceptable in "Decent" Society. If we are not totally stupid and blindly selfish on all possible occasions, we are about as bright and ethical as anybody in history has ever been. The greatest batters in the history of baseball all had batting averages well below 0.500, which means they missed more than half the time they swung. Medieval morality and theology have left us with the hypocritical habit of pretending batting averages close to 0.999 in both knowledge and ethics. (The Absolutists go around talking and acting as if their averages were actually 1.000 or sheer perfection.) On average, I think I score under Babe Ruth, and I suspect you do, too. There thus appears to be a great deal of conceit and self-deception in the habitual poses of intellectual certitude and ethical perfection among the educated classes. It would appear more in keeping with honesty, I think, to recognize, as analogous to Murphy's Law, the unscientific but useful generalization I call the Cosmic Schmuck Principle. The Cosmic Schmuck Principle holds that if you don't wake up, once a month at least, and realize that you have recently been acting like a Cosmic Schmuck again, then you will probably go on acting like a Cosmic Schmuck forever; but if you do, occasionally, recognize your Cosmic Schmuckiness, you might begin to become a little less Schmucky than the general human average at this primitive stage of terrestrial evolution.

So, I do not claim to be either as bright or as "moral" as the authorities on Natural Law. As some variety of Cosmic Schmuck, the best I can claim is that I have developed, over the years, some sense of the difference between real horseshit that you can step in and Ideal Platonic Horseshit that exists, evidently, only in the contemplation of those who worship such abstractions: and I continue to notice that Natural Law bears an uncanny resemblance to Ideal Platonic Horseshit.

# METAPHYSICS WITHOUT "GOD"

*I fear we have not gotten rid of "God" because we
still have faith in grammar.*

—Nietzsche, *The Joyful Wisdom*

Turn we now to the Gentiles. The modern form of the
"Natural Law" mystique is unlike the Catholic dogma in not
invoking "God" *very* explicitly and in becoming civilized
enough not to threaten us with roasting or toasting or
barbecuing or charbroiling if we are heretics. It remains like
the Catholic dogma in attempting to tell us what we *should*
and *should not* do: it wishes to legislate for us, according to
its own Procrustean abstract principles, and it regards us as
scoundrels if we will not obey its dictates. It does not think
that we could or should judge individual cases for ourselves,
and it does not suspect that we might be obliged to do so if we
are not to be total zombies or robots programmed by its
Platonic or extramundane Rule Book.

However, if the Catholic form of "Natural Law" dogma
seems to be based on sheer bluff (on propositions that can
neither be verified nor refuted), the modern version of the cult
seems to be based on total confusion. One knows what the
Catholics mean, even if one doesn't believe a word of it, but it
is nearly impossible to decide if the modern "Natural Law"
mystique means *anything*.

The problem is this: if "Natural Law" in the prescriptive
sense (as distinguished from the descriptive models of science)
does not derive from some "gaseous vertebrate of
astronomical heft" called "God" or "Jehovah" or "Allah" or

22

"Wog the Almighty" or something like that, I cannot imagine what the deuce it does derive from. At this point I can only stand around with my bare face hanging out and make my ignorance public by asking annoying questions, like Socrates, even if this makes Prof. Rothbard want to hit me with a chair.

For instance, "Don't put a rubber on your willy, because God will boil you or broil you for it later" makes perfect sense to me, even if I don't believe it, because it is a law in the normal form of the Statute Laws that we encounter every day. That is, it has the same ideational structure as "Don't smoke pot, because we'll throw your ass in jail for twenty years if we catch you" or "Give us 20 per cent of your income or we'll throw your ass in jail for 30 years if we catch you" or zillions of other brilliant notions Statute Law-makers have created. Both of these typical Statute Laws make sense to me, because I understand what they mean. They mean that some people in a government office want to control my behavior and purloin my assets and are *threatening* me, and control by threat remains as basic to Government as to Theology. I may or may not obey a given statute law, depending on whether it seems reasonable to me or not, whether it makes so much sense that I would do it anyway (with or without a Law), what chance I think the authorities actually have of catching me if I prefer to follow my own judgement, how much of a nuisance it is to obey the more idiotic and impertinent of such laws, etc., but I know who is threatening me and what they are threatening me with.

But if the "Natural Law" cultist *does not explicitly invoke "God" and explicitly threaten me with the super-jail called "Hell, and is not a representative of some Government or other threatening me with the more limited Hells that humans invent and call "jails,"* I fail to make any sense whatsoever out of the statement that something you or I or the bloke leaning against the lamppost want to do is "against the law," or that something none of us want to do and find repugnant is made obligatory by law. *Whose* law? If such a "law" is not explicitly attributed to a *specific* "God" or a specific "Government," then it is not a law in the punitive sense at all. And we have already seen that it is not a law in the metaphoric sense in which the predictions statistically derived from scientific models are loosely called "laws." So what kind of law is it?

And why should we regard it with the *spooky and clearly religious* emotions of "deep belief" and "passion" that Rothbard urges on us?

George H. Smith, to give him credit, does attempt, in his sketch of a possible future argument, to suggest some kind of meaning for such an abstract and unenforceable "law." His sketch of an argument, alas, rests on rather Aristotelian notions of causality in which predictions are either true or false. That is, a "natural law" in Smith's sense would be akin to an absolutely Newtonian scientific prediction and would be equivalent to a kind of practical science, like saying, "if you jump off a tall building without a parachute, you will get hurt."

One trouble with this unexpected and incongruous intrusion of pragmatism into metaphysics, as I see it, is that it takes the spooky religiosity out of Natural Law, opens the matter to debate and discussion, examination of real details of actual cases, how to gauge probable outcomes, etc., and thus approaches real science, almost. This tendency seems to me a step in the right direction, but it relinquishes the metaphysical Absolute Truth that people like Rothbard and Konkin and other metaphysicians are seeking. That which is placed in a practical sensory-sensual space-time context is no longer absolute, but becomes a matter of pragmatic choice, tactics, strategy and the relativity that obtains in all empirical judgements. Briefly: there is no need for "passion" and "deep belief" when confronted with the probable results of jumping off tall buildings; common sense is sufficient. But such cases are extreme, not typical. The typical human choice remains ambiguous — and even its first result does not "justify" or "condemn" it, since its later results remain to be learned. It only takes common sense, not a three-year course in Existentialism, to understand this.

In other words, Smith's Aristotelian either/or logic does not cover most of the issues which Natural Law cultists are eager to legislate upon, since most choices in the real world do not reduce to Absolute Aristotelian true-or-false verdicts but are probabilistic. Most choices in sensory-sensual space-time or ordinary "reality" are not like jumping off tall buildings, but more like deciding between taking a bus or

24

driving in your car; Rothbard's "passions" and "deep beliefs" rather heavily distort your ability to judge the probabilities pragmatically in such daily affairs, and Smith would be better advised to judge them in probabilistic terms than in metaphysical Aristotelian absolutes. A "passionate" belief that it is always better to drive your car than to take a bus can get you in trouble when the car needs repairs. In short, any attempt to introduce a scientific meaning or quasi-scientific meaning into the metaphysics of Natural Law runs aground on the fact that we do not know the definite or final results of most human actions but only their probable and short-term results. It is, for instance, highly improbable that the police will arrest the majority of pot-smokers in any given city on any given day. The attempt to produce a Natural Law on the basis of such probabilities leads to the conclusion (which most young people have already deduced) that you are fairly safe smoking the weed even if there is a law against it. That is hardly the sort of result Smith is looking for, but it is the sort of result one gets if one does try to think scientifically of the statistics of what behaviours lead to what results. In general, most criminals think, within the limits of their intelligence and imagination, of the probable results of their crimes, and the professionals among them, especially in the Mafia and the multi-national corporations, commit their crimes only after they and their lawyers have arrived at the informed opinion that they will evade successful prosecution. Again, that's the real logic of the space-time world of ordinary events that we usually call the real world, but it is not quite what Smith is looking for.

What Smith would like to find, I think, is a pre-quantum, Aristotelian world, unconnected with either science or daily life, in which "cause" and "effect" are metaphysical absolutes and one has 100-percent accuracy in predicting from any cause an inevitable single effect, with no later side-effects. But one only has that in rare and extreme cases, like my example of jumping off a high building. In most of science and most of social life, one only has various probabilities and nobody can ever guess the probabilities correctly all the time.

Here I cannot resist quoting another of the footnotes with which Samuel Edward Konkin III decorated the shorter version of this essay. On the above remarks on probability, he wrote:

> *Wilson does tread dangerously close to sloppy science here; measurements in the micro-level require such probabilistic formulation but scientific laws remain as Absolute as ever — including the Laws of Quantum Mechanics!*

This assertion deserves more than the one meager exclamation point Konkin gave it. I would have given it at least six or seven. Aside from that, I do not see any need for lengthy comment on this religious outburst. The basic papers in the history of quantum mechanics are collected in Mehra's and Rechenberg's *The Historical Development of Quantum Theory*, of which 4 out of the projected 9 volumes are already in print and cover the period 1900-1926 in which the notion of Absolute Law broke down irrevocably. The reader who thinks that Konkin might possibly know what he is talking about can consult the record and learn what has actually happened, namely that the concept of statistical laws, as I have explained it, replaced the Aristotelian myth of absolutes. It sometimes seems that the modern Natural Law cultists have more in common with their medieval Catholic forerunners than is obvious on the surface. They not only want their *tabus* to be Absolute but they also want science to be Absolute again even when it isn't. As for my remarks about the human world: small businesses all seem to know they have to follow "hunches" in gauging probabilities, while major corporations employ computers to estimate the probabilites mathematically, since Konkin's capitalized Absolutes are not to be found normally in sensory-sensual space-time experience, which usually appears a rather muddled and uncertain realm where two-valued Aristotelian choices do not appear with anything like the regularity with which they are produced in the abstract imaginations of Logicians.

But to return to Smith's attempt at Natural Laws based on pragmatic results of actual acts: my objection has been that even if blurry fields like sociology could someday be made as rigorous as mathematical quantum mechanics, it would still yield only probabilities, not the Absolutes (with a capital A) that metaphysical minds like Konkin desire; but in any case the predictions of such a mathematical sociology (with whatever degree of accuracy) about what will happen or will probably happen, are still in an entirely different area of discourse than *tabus* or Divine Commandments about what *should* happen. As Rothbard would quickly tell Smith, any practical (sensory-sensual, space-time world) considerations — e.g. Mr. A decides that in a given town it is not safe to "live in sin" openly, so he and his lover take separate lodgings — amounts to "mere" pragmatism and are not and never can be metaphysical Absolutes. In a bigger town 100 miles away, Mr. A and his lover can live together openly, and in most big towns they can do so even if the lover is the same sex as Mr. A.

It still seems to me that Natural Law in the moral sense means something concrete (if dubious) when a "god" is asserted and a priest-caste are located who can interpret the "will" of that "god," but without such a "god" and such a priest-caste as interpreters, Natural Law becomes a floating abstraction, without content, without threat, without teeth to bite or solid ground to stand on. All the arguments in modern Natural Law theory would immediately make some kind of sense if one inserted the word "God" in them at blurry and meaningless places in the jargon. It seems that the word is left out because the Natural Law cultists do not want it obvious that they are setting up shop as priests; they want us to consider them philosophers.

In sum, I would follow the "laws" of any "god" if I believed that "god" existed and could punish me for dissent, and in prudence I obey the laws of governments when I think they can catch me, or when these laws are not too grossly repugnant to my sense and sensibilities; but when given a choice between the "Natural Laws" of our latter-day prophets and my own judgement, I will follow my own judgement. I trust myself more than I trust them, and, besides, they can do nothing concrete to enforce their dogmas. They are still waving wooden swords to frighten boobs.

# NATURAL LAW AS VENTRILOQUISM

*Pay no attention to that man behind the curtain!*
—Oz the Omnipotent

According to George Smith's neo-Aristotelian sketch of an argument, from scientific predictions about what *will* happen, we can so act that we will obtain "desirable" goals, and that is "Natural Law." Of course, as we have argued, it is impossible to make scientific predictions about most daily-life events, and scientific predictions are not Aristotelian absolutes but only probabilities, and furthermore Mr. Smith has not bothered to define "desirable," so, to be true to the "real" (sensory-sensual, space-time) world, his idea would more reasonably have to be stated as: from attempts at scientific method, we can make guesses about what probably might happen, and can so act that — except for Murphy's Law — we might if we are lucky obtain goals that seem desirable *to us.* There is no guarantee that such goals would seem desirable to anybody else. Leaving that conundrum aside for the moment, it seems to me that in any such chain of reasoning as we advance from scientific predictions to tactical considerations we pass through areas of increasing uncertainty and ambiguity.

It seems that, in honesty, increasing *doubt* should assail us at each step on that path.

It also seems to me that, in honesty, such doubt must be faced squarely and that the "passion" and "deep belief" urged by Rothbard should be discarded as nefarious self-deception.

Only if all doubts, uncertainties and ambiguities are honestly faced, and beliefs are prevented from over-ruling our perceptions of what is happening in space-time, can we have any ground to hope that with each step away from the mathematical theorems where we began we are not wandering further and further into self-delusion. I may appear too cynical, but my hunch is that, in any such moral calculus, each step away from statistical mathematics is a point of vulnerability where we might succumb to *guesses, hunches, wishful thinking* and downright *prejudice.* The only grounds for "deep belief" in such an existential (non-theoretical) context seems to be a deep emotional *need* for belief.

To be clearer: the main reason scientific predictions (miscalled "laws") are so often marvelously useful appears to be precisely that there is no religious attitude of "moral passion" and "deep belief" connected with them in the minds of researchers. They are, on the contrary, regarded pragmatically, tentatively and with cautious skepticism. It is worth considering that this may be the very reason why scientists so often *accomplish what they set out to do,* for good or ill, whereas Ideologists and Idolators of all persuasions spend most of their time doing nothing but engaging in childish arguments or quarrels with other Ideologists who happen to worship other Idols. (I speak here only of the majority of Ideologists in any generation, who never achieve governmental power. What Ideologists do when they do happen to become governments is the principle reason why I agree with John Adams about the close link between Ideology and Idiocy.)

...and at this point in my original article, editor Konkin inserted another footnote, alleging that "faithful ideologists" have never attained power anywhere. That is so wonderful that I almost hate to spoil its beauty by comment; but it has the same structure as the Christian argument that "true Christians" have never done cruel, murderous things like the *alleged* Christians who were responsible for the Crusades, the Holy Inquisition, the witch-hunts, the continued Catholic-Protestant terrorism in Northern Ireland, etc. This appears to be, again, the essentialist argument: what you see only looks like bread, but "in essence" it is the body of Christ. What you see are not true Christians or faithful ideologists, either. True Christians, faithful ideologists and other Aristotelian essences do not exist in this space-time universe, so, of course, I can neither prove nor disprove anything said about them. They remain outside space-time experience, like the Ideal Platonic Horseshit which lacks all the temporal qualities of actual horseshit. I know nothing at all, at all, about such Platonic Horseshit or such Aristotelian essences. When I refer to ideologists, I mean those who have appeared in this space-time world, such as Cromwell and Robespierre and Lenin, and when I refer to Christians I mean the ones in 2000 years of history and Northern Ireland today, because I am writing only about the world of human experience. I leave the metaphysical universes entirely to Konkin, Rothbard and others who are at home in those phantasmal realms. But to return to the main theme:

Let us assume that I am a brighter guy than I think I am, and that my agnosticism is just the result of pathological modesty; I know that seems absurd, but let us follow it for a moment as a *gedankenexperiment.* Let us say that after many decades of arduous study and research, I might actually find what *seems to me* to be a set of rules about the consequences of human actions, not just in the statistical sense of mass consequences (that would be called mere sociology) but, more wonderfully, *Absolute Aristotelian certainties about individual consequences* (that approaches "morality" or at least the Buddhist morality of *karma*). I admit that I would be rather proud of such a job of work, if I accomplished it, but I would still be uneasy about calling my results "Natural Law" and I would not *demand* that people should believe in my work "deeply" and "passionately." I might call my correlations Wilson's Theory ( that's as far as my vanity goes) — I would secretly fear that said correlations might rather be remembered as Wilson's Folly — and I would ask other social scientists to take enough interest in my findings to try to confirm or refute my data. I can't understand why the Natural Law theorists — if they really think they have knowledge in the scientific sense, and are not just rationalizing their prejudices — don't take that modern, scientific and modest attitude. I don't know why they want to hit us with chairs if we question their dogmas.

30

Even in psychology, barely a science at all, there can be found a few statistical generalizations — "laws" of a sort — that have been found consistent by repeated tests in different universities on various continents. These generalizations have been tested because they are written in scientific language, or close enough to scientific language that they can be understood as predicting specific events which can be observed in a laboratory setting. The "Natural Law" theorists never publish any such scientific reports subject to testing and refutation. Like theologians, they seem almost deliberately to avoid any statement concrete enough to be subject to such testing.

At this point I begin to feel a certain sympathy for the most nefarious of all skeptics, the infamous Max Stirner. Whatever else he proves or fails to prove in the long, turgid, sometimes brilliant, sometimes silly text of *The Ego and His Own*, Stirner at least posed a very interesting challenge in asking how much disguised metaphysics appears in philosophers who avoid being explicitly metaphysical. As I have said, "God told me to tell you not to put a rubber on your willy" might be a Natural Law, if such a "god" exists and is not just a hallucination of some kooky celibates, but "My study of the sociological consequences of individual acts demonstrates that you should not put a rubber on your willy" looks, on the face of it, like a theory, a hypothesis, a matter for debate, maybe even an opinion or a prejudice — one has learned to suspect such "sociology" — and it's hard to avoid the Stirnerite suspicion that calling it, or ideas like it, *Natural Law* may represent only an attempt, conscious or unconscious, to elevate a *theory or hypothesis or opinion or prejudice* to some metaphysical level where nobody will dare criticize it, or even think about it.

Here I recall a familiar ritual: the ventriloquist and his dummy. The dummy seems to talk, but we know that the ventriloquist is doing the talking for him. It is amusing to note that many humans achieve a certain dignity or authority (at least in their own minds, and sometimes in the minds of the gullible) by pretending to be something akin to such dummies. The judge, for instance, acts and behaves to give the impression, "It is not I who speak here; it is the Law speaking through me." The priest similarly claims that it is not he who speaks but "god" who speaks through him. Marxists have become very clever at such dummy-logic and seem often to believe genuinely that they do not act themselves but only serve as vehicles through which History acts. Of course, such dummy metaphysics is often very comforting, especially if you have to do something disagreeable or revolting to common human feelings: it must be a great relief to say that it is not your choice but God or History or Natural Law working through you.

Thus, Natural Law seems like a spook in Stirner's sense, a disguised metaphysics in which people can claim they are not rationalizing personal prejudice or doing what they want but are only dummies through which the Great God Natural Law is speaking and acting.

"I want it this way" — "I prefer it this way" — "I damned well insist on having it this way" — all these appear to me as normal human (or mammalian) reflexes, but we have been brainwashed for centuries with the idea that we have no right to want what we want. Even if we rebel against that masochistic Judeo-Christian heritage, it does not seem wise or politic to admit that we want what we want. It seems more impressive and a lot more polite to do the dummy act. It is not that I want what I want, we then say; rather it is that God or History or Natural Law or some other abstraction *demands* that you give me what I want, or at least get out of my way while I go after it.

Politics, as I now see it, consists of normal human and mammalian demands disguised and artificially rationalized by pseudo-philosophy (Ideology). The disguise and rationalization *always* seems insincere when the other guys do it, but, due to self-hypnosis, becomes hallucinatorily "real" when one's own gang does it. I think at this stage of history, the disguise has become obsolete and counterproductive. *Make your demands explicit* (and leave out Natural Law and all Ideal Platonic Horseshit), and then you and the other guy can negotiate meaningfully. As long as both sides are talking metaphysics, each is convinced the other are hypocrites or "damned eejits."

# ON SODOMIZING CAMELS

*What is strong wins: that is the universal law. If only it were not so often what is stupid and evil!*
—Nietzsche, *Notes* (1873)

The suspicion that what is called "Natural Law" may consist of personal prejudice with an inflated metaphysical label pinned on it grows more insidious as one contemplates the fantastic amount of disagreement about virtually everything among the various advocates of "Natural Law."

Prof. Rothbard tells us that this means nothing, because there are disagreements among physicists, too; but I find this analogy totally unconvincing. The area of physics where there is, and has been for three generations, the greatest amount of disagreement is, I believe, quantum mechanics, but the disagreement there appears totally different in kind from the Marx Brothers chaos among Natural Law ideologists. For one thing, the disagreements in quantum mechanics are all about non-physical, almost metaphysical matters. *There is no disagreement about how to "do" quantum mechanics* — that is, what equations to use in making predictions in given situations. The disagreements are all about what the equations "mean" or what verbal forms (philosophies) are most isomorphic with the mathematics of the equations. This is a question that cannot be answered by experiment or observation, and the Copenhagenists (disciples of Bohr) therefore regard it as meaningless, and, as Gribbin points out in his amusing popularization, *In Search of Schroedinger's Cat*, most working physicists, in fact, use quantum math

33

every day without bothering to ask what the equations "mean." The important point, I think, remains that even if nobody in physics knows how to answer those philosophical or metaphysical questions about "meaning," everybody agrees on *how to ask the questions that physics can answer*.

In the area of Natural Law and metaphysical "morality" in general, there is no shred of such agreement about how to ask meaningful questions (questions that can be experimentally or experientially answered) or even about what form a meaningful (answerable) question would have to take. There is no pragmatic agreement about how to get the results you want. There is no agreement about what models contain information and what models contain only empty verbalism. There is, above all, no agreement about what can be known specifically and what can only be guessed at or left unanswered.

The Ayatollah Khoumeni, for instance, has written an authoritative guide to Natural Law according to "Allah," with whom he is allegedly on intimate terms. In this tome, Khoumeni says that a woman may not get a divorce just because her husband is in the habit of sodomizing camels: "Allah" does not permit divorce for such trivialities and, in fact, frowns on divorce in almost all cases. However, later on Khoumeni allows that a woman may get a divorce if her husband is in the habit of sodomizing her brother. Now, I don't know whether this is a Natural Law, or just represents Khoumeni's personal opinions or prejudices, and I don't know of any test or experiment that can determine if it "is" a Natural Law or "is" just the old duffer's private notion, and nothing in Natural Law theory that I have ever read helps me to decide if this doctrine "is" "really" a Natural Law or just Khoumeni's own way of evaluating the relative merits (or demerits) in sodomizing camels as against sodomizing brothers-in-law.

Meanwhile, the Supreme Pontiff in the Vatican, where they gave us that gem about not putting rubbers on our willies, declares that divorce is against "Natural Law" in all cases. It appears quite clear that when the Vatican says "all cases" they mean "all cases." We had a referendum about that in Ireland, where I live, recently, and the Pope's spokesentities (I am trying to avoid the human chauvinism of writing "spokespersons") made abundantly clear that a man could come home drunk every night, beat up on his wife, seduce and sexually abuse their children, give his wife syphilis, and commit any abomination in the pages of de Sade and the Catholic "god" was still against giving the poor woman a divorce. "All cases," to Aristotelians, means "all cases," and thus it includes not only the guy who sodomizes camels but the guy who buggers his brother-in-law as well. Leaving aside the thought that the Ayatollah begins to seem a relative Liberal compared with the Pope, I still don't have a clue as to a scientific test to determine which of these vehement and dogmatic old men might actually know what Natural Law is, or how to be sure they aren't just calling their own prejudices Natural Law.

The Mormon pipeline to "god" brought back the news, when it ran through Joseph Smith, that polygamy is OK; later, the Mormons found a new pipeline, Brigham Young, who brought back the news that polygamy is not-OK. The Arabs haven't heard that news and imagine that polygamy is still OK, while the Vatican's infallible authority insists that monogamy is the only sexual pattern in accord with God's Will and Natural Law. Do any of these people know a damned thing about "Natural Law," at all, at all, or are they just rationalizing their own prejudices?

In California, the majority of the population practice serial polygamy, or one marriage at a time, and most of them think this is in accord with Natural Law or at least with "Nature," except for those who don't get married at all and just live together because that seems even more "natural" to them — after all, in the "state of nature" animals do not hunt up a "priest" to bless them before mating. California "Natural Law" at least resembles nature to that extent.

A prominent American guru, Da Free John, who claims that he not only knows "god" personally but *is* "god," agrees with the Pope in insisting on monogamy among his followers, but says frankly that he (god) doesn't care whether these monogamous couplings are heterosexual or homosexual. The Pope insists that god wants both monogamy and heterosexuality.

The Aztecs, Mayans, Carthaginians and various others sacrificed members of their own community, even of their own family, to the gods. The Druids "only" sacrificed prisoners of war. Hitler sacrificed Jews and gypsies. Almost all governments still insist on the right to sacrifice young males in battle, and it is against the law to run away or resist the draft. Some states and nations believe in capital punishment; others do not. Pacifists are against killing anybody, but not all pacifists are vegetarians. Some quasi-vegetarians will not eat the higher mammals but will eat fish. Pure vegetarians kill vegetables to eat. And so on. And so on.

To compare this ontological spaghetti with the highly technical disagreements in physics seems to me like comparing ten drunks smashing each other in a saloon with the difference in tempo and mood between ten conductors of a Beethoven symphony. Worse: it seems like comparing the aleotoric contents of a junkyard with the occasional disagreement among librarians about where a given book should be classified in the Dewey Decimal System.

But let's hear from Konkin again. In rebuttal to the above he claims that C.S. Lewis demonstrated an "amazing amount of agreement" among various moral codes. This assertion is not an argument, of course, and I invite the reader to investigate Mr. Lewis's books, especially *The Case for Christianity*, in which this point is labored at length. In my impression, Lewis demonstrated only that you can find an amazing amount of similarity between camels and peanuts if you emphasize only the contours of their backs and ignore everything else. In any event, my examples above are not contradicted; and any study of anthropology will bear out the popular impression that just about the only rule all tribes agree on is the one that says people who criticize the rules should be burned, toasted, boiled in oil or otherwise discouraged from such heresy.

Konkin then proclaims, and you have to read this slowly, "Since Wilson does not acknowledge the possibility (!) that Natural Law is simply conceptualization of the objective workings of human action, he cannot consider the possibility that these various religious leaders are *violators* of Natural Law by their subjective impositions." The bracketed exclamation mark is mine; the rest, in all its beauty, is Konkin's. We now see Natural Law as resting on a *possibility*, rather than on the Absolute certitude which Konkin usually claims; but that seems to be a temporary and inadvertent lapse. Of course, I do not deny that *possibility* and very scrupulously did not deny it even in the first draft of this which Konkin published — all I am asking is that somebody should make the possibility into a *probability* (I don't demand certitude in this murky area) by producing a shred or a hint of an adumbration of a shadow of a ghost of something like scientific or experimental evidence in place of the metaphysical, and meaningless, verbalisms Natural Law cultists habitually use. Until they produce some such sensory-sensual space-time evidence, I still say: *not proven*. Their case is logically *possible*, as all metaphysical propositions are possible, in some sense, in some Platonic realm, but they haven't made it at all probable or plausible that these abstractions function in normal space-time, and they certainly haven't produced any evidence to justify the pontifical certitude they always seem to profess.

As for the rest of Konkin's sentence, claiming that all those who have different ideas of Natural Law from his own are "subjective" and thus "violators" of Natural Law, that, again, seems to be mere assertion, not argument. Of course, all the rival Natural Law cultists will say that Konkin is violating Natural Law as *they* understand it, and since there is no experiential-experimental way to judge among any of them, the matter is on all fours with TV commercials where everybody asserts his/her brand is best and all the others are inferior imitations. For those who believe everything they're told, such assertions may be convincing, but I speak for the skeptics and philosophers, who want convincing reasons before they put any credence in a doctrine.

I have certain goals or values; and I admit, frankly, that these goals or values were chosen by me. The Ayatollah and the Pope and the Mormons and Da Free John and Konkin and Rothbard et. al. have their own, different goals and values, but they all assert that these goals are not chosen freely but are dictated by a Higher Power known as either "God" or "Natural Law" or both in tandem. The consequences of this difference seems to be that you can

37

decide for yourself, without fear or intimidation, whether you like my goals or not, but in the case of those who claim to be ventriloquist's dummies for Higher Power, you are subtly discouraged from choice. You *must* agree with them and accept their goals or you are in a state of "sin" or in "violation" of Natural Law and thus you are being browbeaten by guilt into not thinking for yourself and letting these "experts" tell you what is right or wrong for you. (Of course, none of them understand, or can understand, the concrete specifics of a single hour of your life, but they still think they know what you should do in that hour.)

The most astonishing feature of this ventriloquist act — "I am only speaking for some metaphysical entity *above* you" — remains the historical oddity that some who take on this air of Papal Infallibility call themselves libertarians.

# WHAT IS "AGAINST NATURE"?

*One is necessary, one is part of Fate, one belongs to
the whole, one is in the whole; there is nothing
which could judge, measure, compare or sentence
our being, for that would mean judging,
measuring, comparing, sentencing the whole. But
there is nothing beyond the whole.*

—Nietzsche, *Twilight of the Idols*


Even when some Natural Law theorists, like Smith, admit
the vast gulf between scientific (instrumental) generalizations
and their alleged "Natural Laws" or *tabus*, they still
habitually use *language and metaphor that blurs this
distinction* and creates a semantic atmosphere in which they
*seem* to be discussing "law" in the scientific sense. I do not
want to be uncharitable and accuse such writers of
dishonesty, but it certainly appears that their language habits
create confusion, and I suspect that the Natural Law theorists
confuse themselves even more than they confuse their
readers.

The worst source of this semantic chaos appears to me to
be the phrase, "Natural Law," itself, since it is rather grossly
obvious that nothing can ever happen that truly violates
nature, at least as the word "nature" is used in science and, I
daresay, 99 percent of the time in ordinary speech.

As I mentioned earlier, while I was involved in the "Natural
Law" debate in America via *New Libertarian*, I was involved
in two similar debates in Ireland. In the first debate, the
Catholic Church, through every pulpit in the land, was
denouncing the government's attempt to legalize divorce as
"against Nature" and in the second debate, less nationally
publicized, some witches and Druids and neo-pagans were

debating with one another, in a magazine called *Ancient Ways*, about whether machinery and anti-aging research "were" or "were not" against "nature." I created considerable confusion, hostility and incredulity, in both the Catholic and pagan camps, by simply insisting that nothing that happens in nature can be meaningfully said to be "against" nature. It seems to be very hard for Natural Law cultists of all stripes to understand this.

For instance, one shadowy philosopher writing under the name "Peter Z." — and I don't blame him for his near-anonymity; it can be dangerous to be associated publicly with paganism in Holy Catholic Ireland — replied to each of my attempts to explain that nothing in nature "is" unnatural by compiling angry lists of things and events which *seemed to him* "unnatural;" of course, like most persons innocent of neurological science, Peter Z. assumed that whatever seems unnatural to him "really" "is" unnatural. (Natural Law cultists of all stripes share that pre-scientific framework, I think.) The "really" "unnatural" for Peter Z. ranged from cosmetic surgery to television and included most of what has happened since about 1750 C.E. In general, to Peter Z. nature was natural before industrialism and democracy appeared in the Occident but has become unnatural since then. In short, everything he disliked was "unnatural" and "it is unnatural" was in his vocabulary equivalent to "I don't like it."

To say that nothing in nature "is" unnatural is simply to say that nothing in existence is non-existent. Both of these propositions — nature does not include the unnatural, existence does not include the non-existent — are only tautologies, of course, and I do not reify them as Ayn Rand, for instance, habitually reified "existence." I am not saying anything "profound" here; I am merely saying something about semantics and communication. I am asserting that it is impossible to say anything meaningful in a language structure based on fundamental self-contradictions. This is not meant to be a scientific "law" and certainly not a "Natural Law" (whatever that is); it merely appears to be a necessary game-rule of logic and semantics.

The familiar pagan and romantic idea that machines "are" unnatural, for instance, cannot be admitted into logical discourse because it creates total chaos, i.e., destroys the logic game itself. This becomes clear when one tries to think about it, instead of just reciting it as a banishing ritual, as most pagans and romantics do. How does one define "machine" to avoid pronouncing such design-science devices as the spider's web, the termite city, the beaver dam, etc., "unnatural?" Is a chimpanzee "unnatural" in using a *tool* such as a dead branch to knock fruit from a high tree? Was the first stone axe "unnatural?" Are the bridges in Dublin, which the pagans use along with the Christians every day, "unnatural?" When one starts dividing "nature" or existence into two parts, the "natural" and "unnatural," can any line be drawn at all that is not obviously arbitrary and prejudicial? The atom bomb fills pagans (and most of us) with horror, but could it exist if nuclear fission was not a perfectly natural phenomenon?

It seems that when romantics speak of nature, they mean those parts of the universe they like, and when they speak of the unnatural, they mean those parts of the universe they don't like, but there is no possibility of logical or semantic coherence in such arbitrarily subjective language.

This cannot be called a Logical Positivist or 20th Century view; in the 18th Century already, Burke had enough logical clarity to point out, in his polemic against Rousseau, that the Apollo of Belvedere is as much a part of nature as any tribal totem pole. Since classical art is not as well-known today as it was then, Burke's point can be restated thusly: Marilyn Monroe with all her make-up on, the Empire State Building, Beethoven's Ninth Symphony, Hitler's terrible death camps, the moon rockets, Punk hair styles, the pollution of coal-burning furnaces, the lack of pollution in solar power collectors, and anything else humans have invented, whether we find such inventions wonderful or repulsive, must be in accord with the laws of nature in a scientific sense or they could not exist at all. The only things that can be meaningfully said to be unnatural are impossible things, such as drawing a round square or feeding your dog on moonbeams.

It would be clearer if Natural Law cultists gave up on the oxymoronic concept of *"Natural Laws" that can be violated in nature.* The rules they wish to enforce on us do not appear to be laws of nature — which *cannot* be violated and therefore do not need to be enforced — but rather appear to be "moral laws." It makes sense to say "Don't put a rubber on your willy because that's against moral law" (again: whether one agrees with it or not) but one cannot say "Don't put a rubber on your willy because that's against natural law" without getting involved in endless metaphysical confusions and self-contradictions — "the great Serbonian bog where armies whole have sunk," to quote Burke again — webs of words that connect at no point with sensory-sensual space-time experience.

It appears that the reason that the term "Natural Law" is preferred to "Moral Law" may be that many writers do not want to make it obvious that they speak as priests or theologians and would rather have us think of them as philosophers. But it still seems to me that their dogmas only make sense as religious or moral exhortation and do not make sense in any way if one tries to analyze them as either scientific or philosophic propositions.

It proved as hard to communicate this natural science point of view to editor Konkin as it was to communicate it to Peter Z. In his footnote of rebuttal at this point, Konkin instances examples of alleged "Natural Laws" and then engages in some guilt-by-association. He does not attempt at all to reply to my argument itself — that nothing in nature can be called unnatural for the same reason nothing in existence can be called non-existent. As one natural law, Konkin suggests that a society is impossible when no one produces and all consume. I reply that, if true, this would indeed be a natural law in the science of economics but it would have no more *moral* implications than the law of gravity, and that the way to demonstrate it would be to perform experiments, as was done to confirm the relative (statistical) accuracy of first Newton's and then Einstein's formulae for gravity, in contrast to the method of Natural Law cultists, which is to compose verbal (metaphysical) abstractions. However, I doubt very much that this "law" is valid, since a totally automated society seems theoretically possible and might be one in which nobody produces (the machines will do that) and yet everybody consumes. Konkin's second "natural law" is

Heinlein's famous "There ain't no such thing as a free lunch" from the sci-fi novel, *The Moon is a Harsh Mistress.* I think that should be considered a kind of proverb rather than a "law" and one should not use such a metaphor too literally. For instance, all the cultural heritage — what Korzybski called the time-binding activity of past generations — gives us an abundance of metaphorical "free lunches" in the form of roads, bridges, plants in operation, scientific knowledge, existing technology, music, folklore, languages, discoveries of resources, arts, books, etc., etc. If this cultural heritage of "free lunches" did not exist, each generation would start out as poor and ignorant as a Stone Age tribe.

Konkin's attempt at guilt-by-association seems even more amusing to me than his attempt at suggesting scientific laws of sociology. He writes, "I think it only fair to point out that Wilson certainly hangs around mystics a lot more than, say, professional atheist Smith." I will not comment on the similarity to the "logic" of the late Sen. Joseph R. McCarthy (R-Wis.) and I will not even remark that it is news to me that Konkin keeps me under such close surveillance that he knows how much time I spend in the company of "mystics." I will only say the man sounds rather desperate here. Perhaps he was very tired when he wrote that. In fact, I do share space-time with mystics on occasion, and also with occultists and even witches, and also with physicists, mathematicians, biologists, anthropologists, psychologists, psychiatrists, sociologists, writers, actors, nudists, vegetarians, plumbers, grocers, bartenders, homosexuals, left-handed people, atheists, Catholics, Protestants, Jews, Freemasons and I don't know who all. I travel a lot and talk to anybody who might be interesting. If Konkin means to imply that I have contracted some dread mental illness (a metaphysical AIDS perhaps) by not being a philosophical segregationist and only talking to people who already agree with me, I can merely reply that the only way to learn anything, for a person of limited intelligence like me, is to listen to as many diverse views as possible. Metaphysical wizards like Konkin and Rothbard may discover everything knowable about everything imaginable by sitting in their armchairs and "investigating by reason" the ghostly inner "natures" or "essences" of things, but a person of lower intelligence like me only learns a few things in one lifetime and only manages that much by meeting as many people as possible and asking questions of all those broad-minded enough not to hit me with a chair for such inquisitiveness.

To conclude this part of my thesis, if it were possible to violate nature — to perform an act "against nature" — that would be marvelous, and would undoubtedly be a turning point in evolution. It would certainly seem an exciting show to watch, and I would buy tickets to see it. So far, however, everything that has happened on this planet has been in accord with natural laws of physics, chemistry, etc., which have no moral implications and do not need to be enforced or even preached about.

# WHY NOT "VIOLATE" NATURE?

*I pick the goddam terror of the gods out of my nose!*

—J.R. "Bob" Dobbs

Basically, I am skeptical and extremely dubious (not dogmatically denying) about "Natural Law" because I do not possess the *religious* attitude toward nature (with a small *n*, please). An old joke tells of a preacher saying to a farmer, "God has been good to your field." "Maybe so," says the farmer, "but you shoulda seen the place when He had it to Himself." Like that farmer, I am often more impressed by human creative work than by what this planet was like when "God" had it to himself.

Although I do not agree with the almost Manichean attitude of critic Arthur Hlavaty, who regards nature as a combination of slaughterhouse and madhouse *against which,* by great effort, a few human beings have created a few enclaves of reason and decency, I do agree with, e.g., Nietzsche, Lao-Tse and the authors of the *Upanishads,* all of whom held that nature or existence combines so many diverse elements that we cannot judge or measure or compare it with anything, and cannot describe it as a whole except in contradictions. That is, I can only judge *parts* of nature to "be" by my standards "good" or "evil" or "beautiful" or "ugly" etc.; when attempting to contemplate the whole, I can only see good-evil, heat-cold, day-night, beauty-ugliness, wet-dry, light-dark, wisdom-stupidity, creativity-mechanism, organic-inorganic, life-death, etc. —all possible opposites in

45

continuous interaction. Thus, I neither worship nature (existence) pantheistically nor despise it Manicheanistically, but, seeing myself as part of it, claim the same "right" (in quotes, with no metaphysics implied) as any other part of it to make the best of it that I can. In short, I claim the same "right" as a cockroach, a redwood tree, a rat or a whale to adjust and alter the rest of nature (existence) to make it more comfortable for myself, as far as I can do so without becoming so obnoxious to my neighbors that they conspire to repress me.

I think it rather curious, and a variety of metaphysical madness, that the efforts of humans to so alter and adjust existence are denounced as "unnatural" by ecological mystics who never complain that the rat's efforts to better its lot "are" "unnatural." Since neither humans nor rats can actually do anything unnatural, this popular mysticism seems to signify only that some people like rats better than they like humans.

Of course, that's okay with me, too, as somebody's personal prejudice or preference; I am writing in defense of personal choice here (if you haven't guessed that already); I merely object to having personal choices proclaimed as new religious revelations which we all must share or be damned. Personally, I find the anti-rat bias of most people as absurd as the anti-human bias of ecology cultists. The common domestic rat, *mus rattus Norwegicus*, has outsmarted humans for so long, and survived so many human attempts to get rid of her, that I regard this rodent with profound respect, since I'm not sure *I* could survive the combined efforts of so many clever people trying to get rid of me. That's one reason I try to be polite and agreeable to everybody, most of the time, when I'm not at the word processor and carried away by my own rhetoric.

One of the funniest things I ever saw, it seems to me, was a sign in the Lincoln Park Zoo in Chicago, on the cage of the Great Horned Owl. This sign proclaimed that the Great Horned Owl should be considered "a desirable bird" because she eats various critters that are annoying to farmers. I regard this as a hilarious example of unconscious human chauvinism in its assumption that "the desirable" is that which is desirable "to us." One look at the Great Horned Owl was enough to convince me that she would consider herself a desirable bird whether humans think so or not. She has that charming look of total guiltlessness and shamelessness that makes animals so attractive, because nobody has ever convinced them they are sinners and politically incorrect or that their reflexes or whims are against natural law.

On the other hand, the critters who get eaten regularly by the Great Horned Owl will probably never agree that she is a desirable bird. They almost certainly regard her as actively nefarious.

What I am saying here is that nature-or-existence — the sum total of events in sensory-sensual space-time — cannot be judged or evaluated meaningfully. Parts of it can be, and have to be, judged, as one encounters and endures them, and our hard-wired genetic reflexes tell us *most of the time but not infallibly all the time* "Is this good for me or bad for me?" Beyond that reflex level, we have intuitions and reason and feeling, all equally fallible, and nobody I ever met seemed smart enough to know what's good or bad for the life-forms in one county of one state, much less what's best for the universe as a whole. We judge as we choose between alternatives, but all such judgements are limited by the fact that *all would-be judges are involved in the contest.* To be specific, I "judge" the Norway rat as nefarious when it invades my house and I will be severe, even murderous, in my attempts to expel it, but I do not attempt to judge the Norway rat as a species, and I have a suspicion the Norway rat has its own rather strong views about wise guys who stuff brillo in rat-holes, as William Burroughs once noted.

In this evolutionary perspective, which seems to me the necessary view of one who honestly wants to think scientifically, I see no cause to panic at the thought of "violating" nature. Since it is impossible to escape natural law, any alleged violation must be a discovery of a new natural law or a new aspect of an old law. It is in this context that I have often expressed strong agreement with physicist Freeman Dyson's view that we should not accept the deduction from the Second Law of Thermodynamics which tells us the universe is "running down" and that life will someday be impossible. As Dyson says, the only way to find out if that prediction is true is to *try* to refute it, i.e., to seek for ways that might "rewind" the universe to work toward greater order rather than toward greater entropy. Since we have billions of years to work on this problem, before the alleged "heat death of the universe" is expected to occur, despair about the matter seems decidedly premature. To be stopped by the notion that such a project is "against nature" seems to me as superstitious as the views of those who told the Wright Brothers that their airplane was "against nature."

It is for the same reason that I support anti-aging research and the search for longevity, even though many people tell me this is "against nature." Human lifespan was less than 30 years before the Industrial Revolution, and not just due to "high infant mortality." Death was common, not only between birth and 10 years, but between 10 years and 20, and between 20 and 30: if the pox didn't get you, the plague generally would. For the working class, lifespan was still only around 37 years when Engels wrote *The Condition of the Working Class in England.* It was 50 for all classes in the Western democracies by 1900. It now hovers around 73 years, and is increasing. (A 1976 British study found 300 people over 100 years old in the United Kingdom; a 1986 study found the number had increased to 3000.) Each of these quantum leaps in lifespan, since modern technological medicine began, could be denounced as "against nature" just as plausibly as modern longevity research can be so denounced. My view is that if further extension of lifespan does "violate" nature, we can't achieve it, and people don't need to preach against it; but if it does not violate nature, we can achieve it, and I would find it most amusing and entertaining to live 300 or 400 years, or longer. (In that time, I might get smart enough to figure out what the hell is right or wrong for me most of the time, but I think it would take milleniums at least to figure out what the Ideologists all claim to know already, namely what is right and wrong for everybody.) Those who find this appalling to their religious prejudices will forever retain the option of "suicide" (refusal of life-supporting technology) at whatever age seems "natural" to them — at 30 if they think we have only become "unnatural" since the French Revolution, at 50 if they think we only became "unnatural" in this century, etc.

In general — although I love animals and often go into raptures over the singing of birds, and even have a kind of reverence for species who are judged "ugly" and offensive by human chauvinism but still go on living and seemingly enjoying life despite that burden — a great deal of what I admire and appreciate in existence has been the result of human invention and ingenuity, such as pure mathematics and certain music and a few dozen paintings and poems and the "cold inhuman technology" (as ecology mystics call it) that abolished bubonic plague in the last century and allowed me to walk again after I had polio twice and recently (in 1976) abolished smallpox and has made everybody in the Western democracies (even the folks on Welfare) much healthier and more comfortable than most of the people in most of past human history. I, personally, enjoy a good sunset better when I am simultaneously listening to Beethoven or *Carmina Burana* or maybe Vivaldi on that marvelous product of applied quantum mechanics, the modern stereo. Thus, the notion that morality has been, like most of what I love, *invented* by human wit and wisdom does not horrify me, as it appears to terrify Natural Law cultists; it merely adds to my esteem for human beings and the wonderful creativity of the human brain.

At this point editor Konkin added another footnote, which says, in full, "I take no backseat to Bob in cheering sooty smokestacks and their polyvinyl byproducts. Nature-without-(Wo)Man is the ultimate genocide. But that's not why Lawmen oppose the 'human invention' of Natural Law, Natural Rights and morality. One is not ruled by non-contradiction (another statement of Natural Law), one simply must deal with it in order to express one's Will. Make no mistake, if morality is a human invention, *some humans will be enslaved to others.* And that heresy is what we rightly fear." Here Konkin scores a victory, since I certainly cannot rebut this; but that is only because I cannot understand a word of it. I am flattered to be called a heretic, however. Making a wild guess, I hazard that Konkin's first sentence means that the logical law of non-contradiction is a "natural law" rather than a game-rule; in company with most modern logicians, I dissent. Von Neumann's quantum logic seems as valid a game as Aristotelian logic, even though it lacks the non-contradiction rule, and in "natural law" or at least in natural science, this modern 3-valued logic fits atomic physics better than Aristotelian two-valued logic does.

(In fact, as I pointed out earlier, even those unaware of quantum mechanics and von Neumann's math intuitively use a version of his quantum logic in everyday affairs, recognizing that if some predictions appear reliable, and others appear probably totally unreliable, most events remain in the "maybe" category until we encounter and endure them. We only forget this three-valued (yes, no, maybe) logic when hypnotized by Aristotelian metaphysics, and the fact that von Neumann's math, based on three yes-no-maybe truth-values, came as a shock in the 1930s merely indicates that Academia had indeed been hypnotized by Aristotle for over two millenia. No practical person ever believed that daily-life choices could be reduced to Absolute either/or dichotomies.)

How one gets from such technical points in logic theory to Konkin's conclusion that if (and only if?) morality was invented like science and philosophy then slavery can (or must) exist, is a mystery beyond my powers of comprehension. I am a slow learner, as I have admitted. It is my impression that slavery has existed in most pre-industrial societies, was "justified" by whatever philosophy or pseudo-philosophy was handy at the time, and resulted from the lust for profit rather than from philosophical speculation. It is also my impression that the majority of Natural Law theorists in the 18th Century found slavery quite compatible with their ideas of Natural Law, simply by assuming that black people had a ghostly indwelling "nature" or "essence" different from that of white people. Since, like all metaphysics about indwelling spooks or essences, this cannot be proven or disproven experimentally, slavery was only abolished when it became economically less profitable than industrial "free" labour.

I can't resist adding that the word "heresy" is appropriate for Konkin to use in castigating me. The word "heresy" is not only redolent of the medievalism that infests Natural Law theory, but is singularly appropriate for them to use as a cuss-word. It comes from the Greek, *hairesis,* to choose; and that is what this debate is all about. The Natural Law philosophy

50

arose among Christian dogmatists, and those who insisted on their right to choose for themselves instead of accepting "revealed" dogma were naturally called *choosers* or heretics; after nearly 2000 years, the debate still reduces to Natural Law cultists trying to tell the rest of us what is right and proper, and some of us still *choosing* to think for ourselves. (Finally, I do not admire sooty smokestacks; I admire the creative intelligence that has produced non-polluting technologies even though Capital has not yet invested in them.)

Basically, the idea that something is devalued or degraded if it is shown to be a human invention sounds rather medieval and theological to me, and again incites Stirnerite suspicions about the unconscious metaphysical baggage still lurking in the heads of self-proclaimed Rationalists. If Bach invented his music instead of "receiving" it from some trans-mundane or metaphysical source, that does not lessen my love for the music; it merely increases my esteem for Johann Sebastian himself. If Newton and Einstein invented their gravitational models rather than "discovering" them — the Copenhagen view, which is admirably popularized by Bronowski in *Science and Human Values* — that does not decrease the practicality of these mathematical inventions but does increase my awe for the brain-power of Isaac and Albert. And if Jesus invented the admirable remark in *John* 8:7 — which ought to be burned into the backside of every moralist, with a branding iron, since it is the one "moral" idea in human history that they most frequently forget — that does not decrease the wisdom of the saying but adds much to my admiration of Jesus; it still makes sense if he thought of it himself instead of receiving it by psychic pipeline from Papa Tetragrammaton. And, for that matter, if the pyramids were created by people, and not by extraterrestrials as von Daniken would have us believe, that does not change my evaluation of the pyramids but adds further to my esteem for my fellow humans.

In short, I do not think things have to be inhuman to be wonderful, and I do not believe that because something has been produced by humans it is therefore contemptible. Both of these ideas, I suggest, look suspiciously like hangovers from the masochism of medieval monkery.

Before closing this section, it seems necessary to point out the outstanding error of Max Stirner, the first philosopher to realize fully that, while modern Natural Law theory pretends to be rational, it actually carries its medieval metaphysics hidden in blurry metaphors. Stirner proceeded from this discovery, which he documents beautifully and sometimes hilariously, to a rather extreme *non sequitur*, and claims (or in the heat of his rhetoric seems to be claiming) that, if morality is a human invention, morality is somehow absurd. At this point I suspect Stirner also was not free of medieval anti-humanism. I would rather say that because morality appears to be a human invention, we should esteem it as we esteem such inventions as language, art and science. This esteem, readers of this essay will realize by now, does not mean uncritical adulation. Rather the reverse: I believe we express our esteem for the great moralists, poets, artists and scientists of the past by imitating their creativity rather than parroting their ideas, and by *creating* our own unique voices and visions and contributions to humanity's accumulated wisdom and folly. (I always hope to add to our wisdom, but realize that the probabilities are that I am, just as often, adding to our folly.)

It hardly seems necessary to add, at this point, that Hitler thought he was following "Natural Law" when he invaded smaller countries, and although his scientific error can easily be refuted, he seems, in some ways, more realistic and less medieval than most Natural Law mystics. In brief, Hitler thought, as the Social Darwinists of the previous century also thought, that the "cruelty" and "inhumanity" of the animal world means that to be "natural" or to act in accord with "natural law" means to act as mercilessly as a predator stalking and devouring its prey. Since this theory is based on actual observation of actual animals, it sounds more like scientific "natural law" than the metaphysics we have been criticizing.

I do not believe in this form of "natural law" any more than I believe in the others, because "nature" is too complicated and diverse, as I have already pointed out, for any "moral" generalizations to be drawn from it. *Sometimes* evolution rewards the behavior that seems "immoral" to civilized people, as in the predator example, but, just as often,

52

evolution rewards "altruistic" or "moral" behavior: the social animals have survived because their cooperative behavior gives them an advantage. The statement that there "is" no moral law in nature could better be stated as: there is no *one* moral law in nature. Animal behavior includes every possible "moral" and "immoral" law.

More concretely, the predators are indeed part of nature, but they are only *part*. The prey is part of "nature," too, and it is amusing that no Ideologist on record has ever set out to become the prey on the grounds that such is "nature's way." It seems that like Peter Z., the pagan philosopher, most theoreticians pick what they want out of "nature" and call that part the whole. Nature, moreover, offers us many other models beside predator and prey. There is the parenting relationship, in which analogs and perhaps more than analogs of human love are found. There is the "courage" of the baboon pack leader who will throw himself between attacking leopards and the herd he dominates and protects; there is the "cowardice" of the average mammal who will normally run away from any fight that can be avoided. There are parasites and symbiotes, social animals and isolates, cooperative species and competitive species, and even vegetarians and monogamists.

Nature, in short, exhibits endless variety; but human morality was invented, and is re-invented daily, by people making choices. Since heretics are, etymologically, "those who choose," as pointed out earlier, it should be no surprise that we owe most of our evolutionarily recent "moral" ideas to persons who were considered terrible heretics in their own time. It is no accident that the major refrain in the New Testament is the voice of lonely individual judgement set against abstract Rule Books: "It was written in old times...but I say unto you..."

Or as the old hymn says,

> Jesus walked this lonesome valley
> He had to walk there by himself
> Nobody else could do it for him
> He had to do it all alone.

# THE INDIVIDUAL VS. THE ABSTRACT

*The deviants, who are so frequently the inventive and creative spirits, shall no longer be sacrificed; it shall not be considered infamous to deviate from conventional morality; numerous experiments in life and society shall be made; a tremendous amount of bad conscience shall be lifted from the world.*

—Nietzsche, *The Dawn*

I have been arguing that if morality derives, as its etymology suggests — *mores*: the customs of a people — from human creativity or inventiveness or imagination, that is no reason to despise it. (Blake, indeed, thought "imagination" was another name for "god" and many have felt the same way about creativity.)

All products of creativity and imagination are open to criticism, revision, improvement and continued progress. That has been true in every art and science, and it has even been true for morality itself in relatively open societies, despite the fulminations of Natural Law cultists. *No generation knows enough to legislate for all time to come.* Unless we remain open to the process of criticism, correction, revision and improvement, we become, whether we intend it or not, actively reactionary, and our role then becomes that of opposing creativity and the improvement of the human condition.

The attempt to remove moral choice from the realm of humanity and place it in a "spooky" or Platonic superhuman realm, thus, has historically usually been allied with political conservatism and reaction; libertarians who espouse this mysticism should be aware they are using the ammunition of the enemy, which may blow their heads off someday. Since Platonic realms cannot be investigated by sensory-sensual-scientific means, no experiment can refute any doctrine offered about them. The experimentalist can only say, as I do, *unproven*, and perhaps add a few remarks about the "meaningless" nature of propositions that can neither be proven nor refuted. Those attracted to "superhuman" or "transmundane" morality or "Natural Law" or similar metaphysical speculation, therefore, will be drawn chiefly from the ranks of those tempermentally averse to the experimental method, to science, and to "revisionism" in general: those who are seeking an artificial stasis in an otherwise evolving and ever-changing universe. Climbing into bed with a metaphysician means climbing into bed with a reactionary also.

I cannot stress too strongly that, since Platonic realms cannot be investigated by experiment, they are beyond the most powerful critical instrument we possess: a morality so located is beyond normal philosophical analysis or criticism, and akin to the *tabu* systems of savages and organized religion. And, since Platonic realms are usually considered "eternal" or "timeless" or in some way beyond change, adopting this Platonic stance tends to imply that we should go back to the medieval practice of *memorizing* some form of Holy Writ rather than continuing the modern practice of *analyzing* experience itself: this seems psitticine to me.

Finally, since such Platonic realms are alleged to be Absolute, inaccessible and timeless or "eternal" all at once, the kind of "morality" derived, or allegedly derived, from such realms will be *mechanical* and therefore heartless and mindless: the Rule Book tells you what to do. Think of the old farmer throwing Lillian Gish and her baby out in the snowstorm in *Way Down East* and you will have a vivid image of what that kind of mechanical morality has generally meant, why Joyce "feared those big words that make us so unhappy," and why educated people these days almost visibly *cringe*, or at least shrink with "fear and loathing" at the very mention of the word "morality." To be blunt, it stinks of Falwell and Reagan. If libertarianism means anything, it certainly should mean progress, not stasis; change, not medieval dogma; a liberation of energies, not a new cage.

Of course, there is an opinion abroad in the land that libertarianism does mean a mindless, heartless and mechanical system of medieval dogma. I don't know how this impression came about, although it probably has something to do with Randroids and other robot Ideologists who occasionally infest libertarian groups. Frankly, I have always loathed being associated with such types and devoutly wish libertarianism could be sharply distinguished from Idolatry and fetishism of all sorts. If liberty does not mean that we can all be more free, not less free, then I need to find a better word than "liberty" to describe my aspirations; and if we are to be governed by a Natural Law Rule Book of extramundane authority, we can scarcely claim to have advanced beyond the dark ages and might as well make our submission to the Pope again. (He's funnier than Ayn Rand, anyway.)

I do not see this dispute, then, as merely philosophical hair-splitting, and I would hate to see it degenerate into Ideology. I am not claiming to offer Eternal Truth here (I don't know where such a commodity is to be found) but only stating an attitude. If Ideologists ever convince me that this pragmatic, individualistic, scientific attitude is incompatible with libertarianism, then I will find some other name for myself and not use the word "libertarian" anymore. I am not interested in Ideologies and don't give a damn about labels at all, at all. I am interested only in what makes the world a little more reasonable, a little less violent and somewhat more free and tolerant than it has been in the past.

What I am writing about, in fact, might better be called *life-style* than politics. As Tim Leary once said, the only intelligent way to discuss politics is on all fours, since it all comes down to territorial brawling in the end. The questions that I pose are basically matters of lifestyle and almost of *taste:* are we to be self-governors or are we to be ruled by ghostly abstractions from other worlds? Do we dare to trust our own judgements, fallible though they may be, or do we look for super-sensory Authority to decide hard cases for us? Are we willing to learn from others, and from the unique experience of each day, or do we have an abstract blueprint that we never revise? We all have brains which use rational programs to decide cases that can be decided that way, and which also use other circuits loosely called feeling and intuition and memory, and all of these, including reason, can be self-deceptive at times, but if we have a sense of humor and lack a sense of Papal Infallibility, we don't make too many gross errors (most of the time); will we use that bundle of cells in our skull, or will we mechanically look up the answer in the rule book? Are we going to be individualists eventually, or must we always rely on metaphysical abstractions that look suspiciously like theological *tabus* in disguise?

As I say, these are questions of attitude and life-style, not of party politics and Ideology. But they all resolve to the one basic question that separates the sheep from the goats in every generation: are we learning and growing every hour, or are we still enthralled by verbal abstraction, by Ideal Platonic Horseshit that never changes?

# TOWARD A CONCLUSION ALMOST

*It used to be thought that physics describes the universe, but we now know physics only describes what we can say about the universe.*

—Niels Bohr, quoted in Paigels, *The Cosmic Code*

It seems to me that the most important discovery of modern science and modern philosophy is contained in Bohr's distinction (above) between "the universe" and "what we can say about the universe." Bluntly, "the universe" must always be considered somewhat unknown and uncertain, consisting in a sense of two parts:

I. What we can meaningfully say about "the universe" at this date — the results of all human experience and experiment that has been so often repeated that we feel safe in regarding it as not totally hallucinatory.

II. All the rest of existence which has not yet been encountered and endured by humans.

From the "modern" or post-quantum point of view, it now seems clear that the attempt to talk meaningfully about both class I and class II can never succeed; to endeavor to do it all, as Heisenberg said, is like relapsing into medieval debate about how many angels can dance on the head of a pin. Scientifically meaningful speech deals with class I, what has been repeatedly encountered in human experience. Speech about class II does not contain scientific meaning, and it is hard to see what kind of meaning it does contain.

It is often said that post-Bohr physicists "deny reality," and this leads to the impression that they have become solipsists or radical sujectivists. Editor Konkin's footnotes (not all of which I have bothered to rebut, since some appear meaningless to me) contain a strong conviction that my own post-quantum views "are" subjectivist. This seems to derive from another over-simplified Aristotelian dualism — one is *either* objectivist *or* one is subjectivist. Some of us, however, can count beyond two, and see many alternatives where Aristotelians see only digital either/ors.

The post-quantum view is often called *transactional* or *holistic*; either of those labels seems more appropriate than "subjectivist" which chooses one side of an artificial Aristotelian dualism. The transactional view does not require extensive immersion in quantum math; it has appeared independently in psychology and neurology and, especially, perception science. As I continue to point out, most ordinary people, when not hypnotized by a logician or a demagogue, intuitively employ the post-quantum and transactional point of view in daily life.

For instance, we all *hallucinate* occasionally, although we do not think of it that way and generally do not worry about our "mental health" or rush off to a psychiatrist when it happens. I refer to simple incidents like this, which happen every day to most of us: You are walking down the street, and you see an old friend approaching. You are astonished and delighted, because you thought he had moved to another city. Then the figure comes closer, and you realize that your *perception-gamble* (as transactionalists call it) had been in error: the person, as he passes, is clearly registered as a stranger.

This does not alarm you, because it happens to everybody, and daily "common sense," without using the technical terms of quantum physics and transactional psychology, recognizes that perception and inference are probabilistic transactions between brain and incoming signals. Every perception is a gamble, in which we see part, not all, (to see all requires omniscience) and "fill in" or project a convincing hologram out of minimal clues. We all intuitively know the obvious and correct answer to the Zen *koan*,

Who is the Master who makes the grass green?

Perception, as a transaction between brain and signals, contains the same ambiguities as quantum mechanics, we are arguing, because scientific instruments only magnify and make more inescapable the recognition of the transactional nature of knowledge. The laboratory conditions of brain + instruments + signals just makes more inescapable the transactional character of the daily-life experience of brain + signals. We never know "the universe" — a reified abstraction. What we do know, because it is as intimate as our jugular vein, is our transactions involving brain + signals or brain + instruments + signals. This makes the total of "what we can meaningfully say" — namely reports on our transactions with those energies we have tentatively decoded and thus converted into signals.

All such decodings remain tentative, not certain, because we cannot predict future experience and experiment.

The "modern" quantum-psychology view, then, is not subjective or objective, but holistic (including "observer" and "observed" as one synergetic *gestalt*); and it does not "abandon reality" in some mad surrealist excess of solipsism but, more concretely and specifically, redefines "reality," not as a block-like entity "outside" us in Euclidean space — we now know Euclidean space itself is only one model among many — but as an ongoing transaction in which we are involved as intimately as in sexual intercourse.

This intimate involvement may or may not be a scientific equivalent of the Oriental "dance of Shiva," as some popularizers claim, but it smashes down what Dr. J.A. Wheeler calls "the glass wall" which Aristotelian logic tacitly assumes between "me" and "the universe." As Dr. David Bohm points out in *Wholeness and the Implicate Order*, leaving "me" out of the "universe" never corresponded to experience, even when it was a fashionable form of thought, because experience consists of whole transactions (synergies) which, in experience, are never broken but form a seamless unity. My *experience* is *my* experience.

Absolutists of all sorts — not just the Natural Law theorists — have always wanted to abolish disagreements by finding "one truth" valid for all participants in the life experience. Because each brain makes its own transactions with energy, turning energy into such "signals" as it can decode in its habitual grid, this totalitarian dream of uniformity seems neurologically impossible. Each of us "is" the Master who makes the grass green, and each of us makes it brighter or duller green depending on how awake we are or how deeply we are hypnotized or depressed. The case for individualism rests entirely on the fact that, each individual being neurologically-experimentally unique, each individual, however "queer" or "perverse" or "alien" they may seem to local prejudice, probably knows something that no other individual has ever noticed. We all have something to learn from one another, if we stop trying to ram our dogmas down everybody else's throat and listen to one another occasionally.

"Subjectivism," then, applies more to the Absolutists than to modern post-relativity and post-quantum thinkers. The Absolutist has found one way of organizing energy into signals — one model — which has become his or her favorite brain program. This model, being a brain product, retains autobiographical (subjective) elements, and the Absolutist is deluded in projecting it outward and calling it "reality." The "modern" view seems more "objective" in saying, at each point, "Well, that model may have some value, but let's look back at the energy continuum and see if we can decode more signals, and make a bigger or better model." The Absolutist, insisting that his/her current model contains all truth, appears not only more subjective, but unconscious of his/her subjectivity, and thus "bewitched" or hypnotized by the model. In insisting that his "one true model" or Idol should be satisfactory to all other brains, and especially in the favorite Absolutist error of assuming that all other brains which do not accept this "one true model" as the only possible model must be illogical or mad or dishonest and somehow nasty, the Absolutist always tends toward totalitarianism, even in sailing under the flag of libertarianism.

Blake said, "One Law for the Lion and Ox is tyranny." But even more, one "truth" for the Lion and Ox is impossible. There will always be different lanes for different brains, different scenes for different genes, different strokes for different folks.

We can negotiate meaningfully when we understand these neurological facts. When we think we have the "one true model," we cannot negotiate but only quarrel, and, in politics, usually we fight and kill.

# SLEEP-WALKING AND HYPNOTISM

*All that we are is the result of all that we have thought. It is founded on thought. It is created by thought.*

—Gotama Buddha, *The Dammapada*

I stated at the beginning that this booklet concerns hypnosis and self-hypnosis; I shall now explicate that remark.

If you are arguing for racial equality with a man who keeps using the word "nigger," you will eventually discover that you are making no headway and that some barrier prevents clear communication. If you are discussing censorship laws with a lady who keeps using the word "smut," you will experience that same sense of banging your head against a brick wall. If you attempt to reason with a Marxist, the word "bourgeoise" will eventually be invoked to banish any coherence or logic in what you have been saying.

It is a truism in social science that human beings can be defined as the language-using class of life. Buddhists, semanticists and hypnotists know that we not only *use* words but are also easily mesmerized by them. Hypnotists in real life seldom have to use glittering jewels or shining mirrors as they do in films; the ordinary domesticated primate can be hypnotized quite quickly and easily with *words* alone, spoken in proper cadence and with abundant repetition. Advertisers try to hypnotize us all the time, and judging by the fees they collect from satisfied clients, they are doing very well at it. Having used hypnosis in my psychological seminars for nearly 20 years now, I am quite prepared to agree with G.I.

Gurdjieff and Colin Wilson that most people can be said to be hypnotized most of the time, and that the professional hypnotist only switches them from their habitual trance to a different trance.

In fact, when I first started using hypnotism I was astounded that so many people went into deep trance quickly when I was only attempting to induce light trance. It was many years before I understood fully Gurdjieff's insistence that most people are sleep-walking in a deep trance state most of their lives. Now I am only astounded that many people actually come out of their trance often enough to remember, occasionally, what they intended to buy at the supermarket.

If you have to deal with neurotics regularly, you will eventually observe that most of them say *aloud* once or twice a week something to the effect, "They won't give us a chance," "You can't win," "The smart boys have it all sewed up," etc. The odds are that such a neurotic is silently repeating these sentences sub-vocally — in the "interior monologue" of ordinary consciousness — many, many times a day. This form of self-hypnosis is known as a *Loser Script* in the language of Transactional Analysis.

Other people hypnotize themselves into other reality-tunnels by endless repetition of such *mantras* as "I like everybody, and everybody likes me" (the successful Salesman script), "All niggers are treacherous" (the Racist script), "All men are bastards" (the reverse sexist or Radical Lesbian script), "I *deserve* a drink after a morning like that" (the apprentice Alcoholic script), "I can't control my temper" (the Go Directly to Jail Do Not Collect $200 script), "Cancer is only mortal mind. Divine mind has no cancer. I am Divine Mind" (the Christian Science script), etc.

Self-hypnosis need not be destructive, obviously. Like "faith," it can be a releaser of energy, a spur to creativity and a tool of self-improvement (metaprogramming the human biocomputer) — as long as you're not a damned fool about it, to quote the immortal W.C. Fields again.

Uncovering the sentences that perpetuate self-hypnosis is a major goal in some forms of psychotherapy — such as Rational-Emotional Therapy, Reality Therapy and

Transactional Analysis — and is acknowledged as important in most other forms of psychotherapy. Many accelerated forms of therapy now in vogue rely largely on teaching people to abandon *negative self-hypnosis* and begin using the powers of *positive self-hypnosis.*

Count Korzybski, the pioneer semanticist, said that humans are the symbol-using species and therefore those who control symbols control human destiny. Stokely Carmichael, a Black civil rights leader of the 1960s, said it this way: "The power to define is the power to control."

Hypnotism can induce people to shut off pain at the synapse, and surgeons can operate on them as if they were anesthetized. Hypnotism can stop bleeding. Hypnotism can even induce hallucinations: "In five minutes," the hypnotist says, "you will see a clown stick his head in the window." In five minutes, the subject looks startled and giggles, then reports that he saw a clown at the window. Advertisers have learned this trick, also. Most men have a favorite brand of beer which they insist tastes better than others, but when blindfolded, as Packard documented in *The Hidden Persuaders*, these men cannot identify their favorite brand from a selection of five. The superior taste they ordinarily experience must be considered a hypnotically induced hallucination.

I have always dreaded both Ideology and Theology, because they make people cruel. It now appears to me that ordinary men — and occasionally ordinary women — do monstrous things for their Ideologies and Theologies only because politics and religion function largely, like advertising, through hypnotism and self-hypnotism. This is the opinion also of Colin Wilson in his extraordinary and terrifying *Criminal History of Mankind*. Examining the blood-curdling acts of both those who have always been called criminals (the free-lance marauders) and those government officials who have only been identified as criminals (that is, as "war criminals") in the last generation, Colin Wilson concludes that in each case there is abundant evidence that the perpetrators of atrocities were, not metaphorically but literally, hypnotized or self-hypnotized. That is, they had learned how to make hypnotic words and sentences more real to their brains than the ordinary testimony of the senses and feelings.

This seems hard to believe at first, as it is hard to believe that most people are hypnotized most of the time. But consider two of the outstanding forms of Ideology in the world — racism and sexism. If you have observed a racist or sexist in action, you will note that they do not see or observe the concrete human being before them; they "see" only the hallucination triggered by the hypnotic words of their internal racist or sexist script, which they have been repeating, both aloud and sub-vocally, for many, many years. This, of course, is easiest to observe when you are the victim of racism or sexism, but, fortunately for our species's education there is enough reverse racism and reverse sexism around these days that I can confidently expect all readers have had a few experiences with deeply hypnotized subjects of the type I am describing. Even if you are white, you have encountered black racism and observed that it doesn't react to your sensory-sensual activity in space-time at all: it is a robot program that reacts only to your skin color. You might have learned from that what it is like for black people to try to deal with thoroughly hypnotized white racists. And if you are male, you have undoubtedly met a few deeply hypnotized Radical Feminists by now, and have some clue as to how women feel in dealing with male sexism.

Every Theology and every Ideology, it seems to me, is an endeavor in hypnotism and self-hypnotism. If there is one thing that everybody knows in common sense — when they are in "their right minds" and not hypnotized — it is that "all generalizations are hazardous" and that individual cases are each unique. The function of Theological and Ideological hypnosis is to forget this common sense and follow a robot-program that evades the responsibility of thinking and feeling anew in each unique situation. It is not just the other gang's Theology or Ideology that is nefarious: all Theology and Ideology is nefarious. It is a form of sleep-walking in which we can do monstrous things because we are not alive, awake and aware of who we are, where we are and what is going on around us.

In hypnosis, we "live in our heads" — i.e., in the "magic" verbalisms that induce and perpetuate our trance. In

65

hypnotism, if we believe pain does not exist, pain goes away, and if we believe a disciplined German officer should not have normal human feelings, normal human feelings go away and we can perform atrocities. In hypnotism, any verbal formula can become as "real" as or even more "real" than the sensory-sensual manifold of space-time. In hypnosis, a verbal abstraction such as Racial Purity or Class War or God's Will becomes more "real" and more "important" to the brain than the sense-data reporting a bottle of beer and a ham sandwich on the table or a bleeding victim of the Ideology lying in the street.

The Ideology of Natural Law, I submit, must be classed as a form of self-hypnosis. I have argued, throughout, that the Platonic world of Natural Law and other abstractions does not interface at any point with the space-time continuum of ordinary sensual-sensory experience, the bottle of beer or the victim's body. For this reason, which they know, the more intelligent Natural Law theorists attribute Natural Law to some other, allegedly "higher" world. I suggest that where Natural Law exists — where gods and demons and faery-folk and *pookahs* exist — is in the hypnotized brains of those who have invoked these ghostly entities by repeating hypnotic chants to themselves, over and over, until this made-up world is more real to them than the world of experience.

That the Ideologist "lives in his head" is familiar folk wisdom, but it contains terrifying implications.

I have argued that morality derives from human experience, human reason, human feeling, human intuition and human creative energy generally. Other animals do not have "morality" for the same reason they do not have art or science: their brains do not abstract higher-order information from sensory information, as ours do, and hence they do not perform creative acts with information. If this analysis has any truth, then morality, like art and science, is *not a finished product* but almost an *evolving* organism, to which each of us can contribute if we "live with integrity" in Bucky Fuller's sense of that phrase — namely, if we come out of our heads, out of our abstractions, and look concretely at our concrete *individual* experiences in space-time as processed by our *individual* reason and feelings and intuitions. Living with integrity in that sense was once defined by Confucius as "respecting one's own nose." To me, this is what individualism and libertarianism are all about. *"Smash, smash, smash the old tablets of law and wake from the myths that all generations have believed!"*

*If we do not wake up* in that concrete sense — if we are still hypnotized by spooks and abstractions — no manner of talk and chatter about individualism and liberty has any concrete existential meaning, because we are still walking around in a trance: zombies programmed by whatever verbalism in our head stands between us and the thunderous astonishment of every unpredictable moment in waking life.

These ideas can be made more concrete with a parable, which I borrow from John Fowles's wonderful novel, *The Magus.*

Conchis, the principle character in the novel, finds himself Mayor of his home town in Greece when the Nazi occupation begins. One day, three Communist partisans who recently killed some German soldiers are caught. The Nazi commandant gives Conchis, as Mayor, a choice — either Conchis will execute the three partisans himself to set an example of loyalty to the new regime, or the Nazis will execute every male in the town.

Should Conchis act as a collaborator with the Nazis and take on himself the direct guilt of killing three men? Or should he refuse and, by default, be responsible for the killing of over 300 men?

I often use this moral riddle to determine the degree to which people are hypnotized by Ideology. The totally hypnotized, of course, have an answer at once; they *know beyond doubt what is correct, because they have memorized the Rule Book. It doesn't matter whose Rule Book they rely on — Ayn Rand's or Joan Baez's or the Pope's or Lenin's or Elephant Doody Comix* — the hypnosis is indicated by lack of pause for thought, feeling and evaluation. The response is immediate because mechanical. Those who are not totally hypnotized — those who have some awareness of concrete events of sensory space-time, outside their heads — find the problem terrible and terrifying and admit they don't know any "correct" answer.

I don't know the "correct" answer either, and I doubt that there is one. The universe may not contain "right" and "wrong" answers to *everything* just because Ideologists want to have "right" and "wrong" answers in all cases, anymore than it provides hot and cold running water before humans start tinkering with it. I feel sure that, for those awakened from hypnosis, every hour of every day presents choices that are just as puzzling (although fortunately not as monstrous) as this parable. That is why it appears a terrible burden to be aware of who you are, where you are, and what is going on around you, and why most people would prefer to retreat into Ideology, abstraction, myth and self-hypnosis.

To come out of our heads, then, also means to come to our senses, literally — to live with awareness of the bottle of beer on the table and the bleeding body in the street. Without polemic intent, I think this involves waking from hypnosis in a very literal sense. Only one individual can do it at a time, and nobody else can do it for you. You have to do it all alone.

# YOU WILL ALSO WANT TO READ: